OXFORD ENGLISH MONOGRAPHS

Young Coleridge and
the Philosophers of Nature

IAN WYLIE

CLARENDON PRESS · OXFORD
1989

Oxford University Press, Walton Street, Oxford OX2 6DP
Oxford New York Toronto
Delhi Bombay Calcutta Madras Karachi
Petaling Jaya Singapore Hong Kong Tokyo
Nairobi Dar es Salaam Cape Town
Melbourne Auckland
and associated companies in
Berlin Ibadan

Oxford is a trade mark of Oxford University Press

Published in the United States
by Oxford University Press (USA)

British Library Cataloguing in Publication Data
Wylie, Ian
Young Coleridge and the philosophers of
nature. —(Oxford English monographs).
1. Poetry in English. Coleridge, Samuel
Taylor. Special themes: Science — Critical
studies
I. Title
821'.7
ISBN 0-19-812983-1

Library of Congress Cataloging-in-Publication Data
Data available

Phototypeset by Dobbie Typesetting Limited
Printed in Great Britain
at the University Printing House, Oxford
by David Stanford
Printer to the University

To Charles Ronald and Margaret Wylie

Contents

Abbreviations

The following abbreviations are used throughout:

BL	British Library
BLB	George Whalley, 'The Bristol Library Borrowings of Southey and Coleridge, 1793–98', *The Library*, 5th ser., iv (1949), 114–32.
CL	*Collected Letters of Samuel Taylor Coleridge*, ed. Earl L. Griggs, 6 vols. (Oxford, 1956–71).
CN	*The Notebooks of Samuel Taylor Coleridge*, ed. Kathleen Coburn, 3 vols. (London, 1957–).
CUL	Cambridge University Library.
The Friend	Coleridge, *The Friend* (1809–10, 1812, 1818), in *The Collected Works of Samuel Taylor Coleridge*. Vol. iv (2 parts). Ed. Barbara Rooke (London and Princeton, NJ, 1969).
JHI	*Journal of the History of Ideas.*
J. Hist. Med.	*Journal of the History of Medicine.*
J. Warburg & Courtauld Inst.	*Journal of the Warburg and Courtauld Institutes.*
Lectures 1795	Coleridge, *Lectures 1795 On Politics and Religion*, in *The Collected Works of Samuel Taylor Coleridge*. Vol. i. Ed. Lewis Patton and Peter Mann (London and Princeton, NJ, 1971).
Memoirs of the Lit. & Phil.	*Memoirs of the Literary and Philosophical Society of Manchester.*
Phil. Trans.	*Philosophical Transactions of the Royal Society of London.*
Poems 1797	*Poems, by S. T. Coleridge, Second Edition. To which are now added Poems by Charles Lamb, and Charles Lloyd* (1797).

Priestley, *Works*	*The Theological and Miscellaneous Works, etc., of Joseph Priestley, LL.D. F.R.S. etc. with notes, by the editor,* ed. John T. Rutt, 25 vols. (1817–31).
'Rugby MS'	Coleridge, holograph manuscript of items published in *Poems on Various Subjects* (1796); formerly at Rugby School, now at the University of Texas at Austin.
Trans. Amer. Phil. Soc.	*Transactions of the American Philosophical Society.*
Univ. Birm. Hist. J.	*University of Birmingham Historical Journal.*
The Watchman	Coleridge, *The Watchman,* in *The Collected Works of Samuel Taylor Coleridge.* Vol. ii. Ed. Lewis Patton (London and Princeton, NJ, 1970).

Unless indicated, all references to Coleridge's poetry are to *Coleridge: Poems*, ed. John Beer (London, 1963). The text of *Religious Musings* used in the reading of the poem in Chapter 6 is taken from the first edition of *Religious Musings* in *Poems on Various Subjects* (1796).

Introduction

1. The Fall

> The present age will hereafter merit to be called the Age of reason, and the present generation will appear to the future as the Adam of a new world.
>
> Paine, *Rights of Man*

On 20 February 1773, at the age of 30, the French chemist Antoine-Laurent Lavoisier wrote in his laboratory notebook: 'I will give an account of all that has been discovered about the air that is given off and taken up by bodies. The importance of this obliges me to repeat all the experiments, because it seems that it will bring about a revolution in physics and chemistry.'[1] Fifteen years later, in March 1789, he published the results of this work in *Traité Élémentaire de Chimie, présenté dans un ordre nouveau et d'après les découvertes modernes*. His book destroyed the old system of 'phlogiston' chemistry and founded the modern science. Four months after its appearance the destruction of the Bastille signalled the end of the *ancien régime* in Europe.

Recalling this time and his radical youth, the middle-aged Poet Laureate of England Robert Southey wrote to Caroline Bowles: 'few persons but those who have lived in it can conceive or comprehend what a visionary world seemed to open upon those who were just entering it. Old things seemed passing away, and nothing was dreamt of but the regeneration of the human race.'[2]

Six months after the Fall of the Bastille, Erasmus Darwin, the doctor-poet of Derby wrote to his friend the great Scottish engineer James Watt: 'Do you not congratulate your grand-children on the dawn of universal liberty? I feel myself becoming all french both in

---

[1] Lavoisier's memorandum for '20 February 1772' (actually 1773), quoted in H. Guerlac, *Lavoisier: The Crucial Year* (Ithaca, NY, 1961), 230.
[2] *The Correspondence of Robert Southey with Caroline Bowles*, ed. E. Dowden (1881), 52.

chemistry and politics.'[3] A month later, in a letter to Benjamin Franklin Lavoisier gave a concise account of his chemical revolution and then turned to politics: 'After you have heard all that has happened in chemistry, I must now tell you about our political revolution. We think that all is now settled, and there is no chance of returning to the ancient order.'[4] What Southey later saw as an age of renewal, Tom Paine and Lavoisier believed to be a complete break with the past.

By 1793 Joseph Priestley, whose chemical genius and blunders had been the inspiration for Lavoisier, could declare in a letter to the Jacobin leaders of the French Revolution that 'with respect to philosophy, and especially chemistry . . . the age of mystery and deception . . . is now over, and rational and useful science has taken place of solemn pretensions, absurd systems, and idle tricks.'[5] In Bristol a young radical, the lecturer, journalist, and poet Samuel Taylor Coleridge, paid homage to 'the Chemist, whose faculties are swallowed up in the great task of discovering those perfect laws by which the Supreme Wisdom governs the Universe!'[6] Two years after the publication of *Traité Élémentaire* Lavoisier declared in a letter to a fellow chemist, Chaptal: 'I am overjoyed that the principles of chemistry I laid down have been accepted. . . . All the younger generation have adopted the new theory, and I have concluded that the revolution in chemistry has now occurred.'[7]

On 8 May 1794, Lavoisier was summoned before the Revolutionary Tribunal as Farmer-General of Taxes, accused of plotting with the enemies of France to overthrow the government. Pleas for clemency on the grounds of his outstanding scientific achievements for France were dismissed with the legendary remark by Coffinhal, President of the Tribunal: 'The Republic has no need of *savants*, it is necessary for justice to be done.'[8]

Antoine Lavoisier was guillotined later that day.

---

[3] Letter of 19 Jan. 1790: *The Letters of Erasmus Darwin*, ed. D. King-Hele (Cambridge, 1981), 200.

[4] Quoted in I. B. Cohen, 'The Eighteenth-Century Origins of the Concept of Scientific Revolution', *JHI* xxxvii (1976), 283.

[5] *Works*, xxi. 88.   [6] *The Watchman*, 34.

[7] Quoted in E. Grimaux, *Lavoisier 1743–1794* (1888), 126.

[8] Coffinhal's infamous remark appears in an address given by the chemist Antoine de Fourcroy, published as *Notice sur la Vie et les Travaux de Lavoisier, précédée d'un discours sur les funérailles, et suivie d'une ode sur l'immortalité de l'âme* (l'an quatrième [1796]), 46.

2. A Bridge Too Far

They still like to pretend that the traditional culture is the whole of 'culture', as though the natural order didn't exist. As though the exploration of the natural order was of no interest either in its own value or its consequences. (C. P. Snow, *The Two Cultures and the Scientific Revolution*)

In 1815 Coleridge, a middle-aged literary giant, looked back in his *Biographia Literaria* on his early literary endeavours. He recalled his first collection of poetry, *Poems on Various Subjects* published in 1796, and remembered how well the critics had received his poems, because they seemed to promise better things to come. The main criticism was the obscurity of the pieces, particularly the longest poem in the collection, *Religious Musings*. Coleridge had defended himself: 'Satisfied that the thoughts, such as they were, could not have been expressed otherwise, or at least more perspicuously, I forgot to inquire, whether the thoughts themselves did not demand a degree of attention unsuitable to the nature and objects of poetry.'[9] We may judge this for ourselves. Here is the poet's précis at the opening of *Religious Musings*:

Introduction. Person of Christ. His Prayer on the Cross. The process of his Doctrines on the mind of the Individual. Character of the Elect. Superstition. Digression to the present War. Origin and Uses of Government and Property. The present State of Society. French Revolution. Millenium. Universal Redemption. Conclusion. (*Religious Musings*, 'Argument')

In the summer of 1795, six months after leaving Cambridge, the twenty-two-year old Coleridge had begun to write complex metaphysical poetry that is almost unparalleled in modern times. A typical passage from this important period is this draft of an 'Effusion' that later became the celebrated poem 'The Eolian Harp':

> And what if All of animated Life
> Be but as Instruments diversly fram'd
> That tremble into thought, while thro' them breathes
> One infinite and intellectual Breeze?
> And all in different Heights so aptly hung,
> That Murmurs indistinct and Bursts sublime,
> Shrill Discords and most soothing Melodies,
> Harmonious from Creation's vast concent?
> Thus *God* would be the universal Soul,

[9] *Biographia Literaria* (1817), ed. J. Shawcross, 2 vols. (Oxford, 1907), i. 2–3.

> Mechaniz'd matter th'organic harps,
> And each one's Tunes be that, which each calls *I*.
>
> (Rugby MS, fols. 31-2)

The young Coleridge was trying to communicate high metaphysical truths in poetry. For seven years Coleridge wrote substantial poetry, and even after he stopped in 1802, he continued to hope that where he had failed, his friend Wordsworth would succeed and write a large-scale philosophical poem.

Yet towards the end of his creative period, Coleridge voiced a fear about the contradiction between poetry and philosophy that has been echoed and accepted by many. In a letter of February 1801 to Thomas Poole, the tanner of Nether Stowey, Coleridge wrote about a conversation with the young chemist Humphry Davy: 'Davy in the kindness of his heart calls me the Poet-philosopher,' he told Poole: 'I hope, Philosophy & Poetry will not neutralize each other, & leave me an inert mass.'[10]

Believing that poetry and philosophy are indeed in conflict, many have argued that this was soon to happen to Coleridge. In the year that *Biographia Literaria* was published, Keats toasted Newton and the confusion of mathematics in the company of Lamb and Wordsworth. He later wrote the famous denunciation of Newton's philosophy:

> Do not all charms fly
> At the mere touch of cold philosophy?
> There was an awful rainbow once in heaven:
> We know her woof, her texture; she is given
> In the dull catalogue of common things.
> Philosophy will clip an Angel's wings,
> Conquer all mysteries by rule and line,
> Empty the haunted air, and gnomed mine—
> Unweave a rainbow . . .
>
> (*Lamia*, ii. 229-36)

These lines were quoted to the present writer when he began undergraduate studies in philosophy, for this age seems to agree with the poets: philosophical notions only distract the creative spirit.

The influential Coleridge critic John Livingston Lowes encouraged this view of Coleridge's work in his classic study *The Road to*

---

[10] *CL* i. 668-9.

Xanadu: A Study in the Ways of the Imagination. Writing of
Coleridge at about the time he completed *Religious Musings*, Lowes
commented: 'Coleridge the poet was still struggling, like a limed bird,
in the clutches of Coleridge the metaphysician. The sure flight of
his imagination when no abstract speculations clogged its wings was
yet to come.'[11]

Coleridge's 'metaphysical' preoccupations at the time were the
philosophies of Newton, Locke, Berkeley, and Priestley. The notion
that these early struggles with empiricism detracted Coleridge from
writing good poetry has gained distinguished modern supporters.
In *Coleridge and the Pantheist Tradition* Thomas McFarland wrote:
'A Newton may do much for the poet as physicist, but he does little
or nothing for the poet as poet.'[12] Owen Barfield echoed this in
What Coleridge Thought: 'Laws of nature . . . are the special
province, not of the philosopher and still less of the poet, but of the
scientist.'[13] Science, or, as Coleridge knew it, 'natural philosophy',
is believed to be a prosaic affair from which the poet can draw
nothing.

Coleridge himself is in part the originator of this view. Deeply
interested in the natural philosophy of the followers of Newton and
Locke, he began to criticize the 'little-by-little' approach to knowledge
a few days after writing one of the great visionary poems of the
English language, *Kubla Khan*:

—I can *at times* feel strongly the beauties, you describe, in themselves,
& for themselves—but more frequently all *things* appear little—all the
knowledge, that can be acquired, child's play—the universe itself—what
but an immense heap of *little* things?—I can contemplate nothing but parts,
& parts are all *little*—!—My mind feels as if it ached to behold & know
something *great*—something *one* & *indivisible*—(letter to John Thelwall,
October 1797; *CL* i. 349)

Writing to Thomas Poole at the same time, Coleridge continues by
attacking the empiricists:

—Those who have been led to the same truths step by step thro' the constant
testimony of their senses, seem to me to want a sense which I possess—
They contemplate nothing but *parts*—and all *parts* are necessarily little—and
the Universe to them is but a mass of *little things*. (*CL* i. 354)

---

[11] 2nd edn. (1930), reprinted (1955), 71.
[12] (Oxford, 1969), 122.   [13] (Oxford, 1972), 131.

Yet although he is critical of the followers of Newton, Coleridge has not rejected their philosophy. Not until the latter part of his German studies in 1799 did he express 'discontent' with the material pantheism of Joseph Priestley; two years later, in the famous set of letters to Josiah Wedgwood on the activity of the mind in the writings of Descartes and the ancients, Coleridge is still criticizing, rather than rejecting, the philosophy of Locke. An unequivocal rejection of the empirical method eventually came in a letter to Poole of March 1801:

> If I do not greatly delude myself, I have not only completely extricated the notions of Time, and Space; but have overthrown the doctrine of Association, as taught by Hartley, and with it all the irreligious metaphysics of modern Infidels—especially, the doctrine of Necessity. (*CL* ii. 706)

Released after half a lifetime in the clutches of this philosophy, Coleridge indulged in some nose-thumbing at its greatest exponent: 'I believe the Souls of 500 Sir Isaac Newtons would go to the making up of a Shakspere or a Milton.'[14] Twice he begged Poole to destroy this remark, but the pleas were ignored by his friend and also by the legion of critics who have taken this comment to be the definite statement through his life of Coleridge's attitude to the founder of modern science.

In his influential book *The Active Universe: Pantheism and the Concept of Imagination in the English Romantic Poets* H. W. Piper wrote of how 'Coleridge in his Unitarian days as well as later opposed Newton's ideas vigorously.'[15] A decade later Norman Fruman asserted that 'very early in Coleridge's writing appears a violent antipathy to Isaac Newton and all his works'.[16] Ten years later two critics, writing from very different perspectives, concur with these judgements. Trevor Levere, writing from the vantage-point of a historian of science, treats Coleridge's early thought on Newton as superficial and uncritical: 'The more Coleridge looked into Newton's work, the less he thought of him.'[17] Kathleen Wheeler, in *The Creative Mind in Coleridge's Poetry*, ends her opening discussion on associationism with the extraordinary conclusion that 'the poetry of this period [the 1790s] is . . . largely free of the constraining

---

[14] Letter of 23 Mar. 1801; *CL* ii. 709.   [15] (London, 1962), 11.
[16] *Coleridge: The Damaged Archangel* (New York, 1971), 131.
[17] *Poetry Realized in Nature: Samuel Taylor Coleridge and Early Nineteenth-Century Science* (Cambridge, 1981), 26.

effects of the "Mechanic Philosophy".'[18] Of the major modern critics of Coleridge John Beer is almost alone in treating Coleridge's many positive references to Newton with any seriousness, though Kathleen Coburn, Lewis Patton, and Peter Mann have stressed in the editions of *CN* and *Lectures 1795* the importance of his scientific reading.

The impression given by many commentators on Coleridge's early thought is that the young poet was 'seduced' by the philosophy of Newton, Locke, and Hartley, his critical faculties not being sufficiently developed to defend him against their superficial charm. Suggestive language can support this view. John Spencer Hill wrote in *A Coleridge Companion* that in 1795–6 'Coleridge was still a Necessitarian *under the spell of* the empirical philosophy of Locke and Hartley.'[19]

The student of Coleridge is thus invited to place his interest in natural philosophy alongside other youthful occupations: radical lecturing and pamphleteering, Utopian colonialism, heterodox faith. Science can have had no part in the development of Coleridge as a great poet. Levere here speaks for many: 'Newton, Hartley, and Priestley together could be made to furnish a philosophical foundation for Unitarianism and for libertarian politics.'[20] True enough: but was that all that was on Coleridge's mind in 1795–7?

The middle-aged Coleridge must take much of the blame for this attitude to his 1790s studies. In *Biographia Literaria* and elsewhere Coleridge made frequent attempts to make light of the young radical of 1795–7, leading many to believe that his studies of that time were not sufficiently deep to influence his finest poetry. Basil Willey stated this eloquently when in 1949 he wrote how 'the enthusiasms of this period were largely froth upon his mind's surface'.[21] Earlier, Shawcross in his 1907 introduction to *Biographia Literaria* found another reason why the mechanical philosophy could not sustain the poet:

Now, that poetry and philosophy, if their message be true, must be founded in the same spiritual experience, Coleridge would have readily acknowledged; indeed, it was the truth for which he had been contending throughout his life. . . . It was the conviction that in either case the whole

---

[18] (London, 1981), 16.   [19] (London, 1983), 25: my emphasis.
[20] *Poetry Realized*, 14.
[21] *Nineteenth-Century Studies* (London, 1949), 7.

self must be active in the apprehension of reality, which in the first instance
opened his eyes to the error of the empiricists in their one-sided interpretation
of a partial aspect of things. (pp. lxiv–lxv)

Kathleen Wheeler developed a similar argument for our age:

What seems inconsistent in the poetry with the determinism and mechanistic
theory of a passive mind inherent in Hartley's Associationism, to which
Coleridge was attached in the 1790s, is the general commitment to the
creativity of mind and to an organic view of reality suggested in the poems
by virtue of their structure and unifying techniques. (*The Creative Mind*, 4)

These arguments sound persuasive: Coleridge could not seriously
have adopted mechanical philosophy and the passivity of mind when
only a dynamic and active mind could have written such poetry as
Kubla Khan and *The Ancient Mariner*. Both critics, however, are
labouring under the same fallacy. Confusing how the mind thinks
with what the mind is thinking about, they assert that it is self-
contradictory for a creative, synthesizing author to conceive of the
passivity of mind. Yet the mechanisms of thought may be passive,
while the thought itself is the active, creative vision of a Coleridge
poem. The error is similar to Berkeley's famous mistake in *Three
Dialogues between Hylas and Philonus* that it is self-contradictory
to imagine a tree which is unconceived: it is the idea which is
conceived, not the tree itself.

Shawcross and Wheeler lay bare an attitude which has been
widespread among critics and has led to some curious statements
on the relative importance of the influences on Coleridge's major
poetry. Many have dismissed the importance of the empirical
tradition because it was a youthful preoccupation of the poet, yet
have written about the profound and lasting influence of Platonism
on Coleridge, because he studied its mysteries at Christ's Hospital!
Even Beer in *Coleridge the Visionary* set the 'mechanistic philosophy
of Locke and Hartley' against Lamb's romantic picture of the
schoolboy intoning 'the mysteries of Jamblichus, or Plotinus'.[22]

Not only is the 'youthful' argument here paradoxical—Platonism
is *early* and thus fundamental, empiricism is *youthful* and thus
ephemeral—but the assertion that empiricism could not have
influenced the creative poet stubbornly fails to acknowledge the fact
that almost all of Coleridge's substantial poetry was written when

[22] (London, 1959), 46.

he was studying the empiricists, and that after his conversion to Kant and the critical philosophy little of poetic substance emerged. Someone who read the above passage from Shawcross without knowing the date of 'The Eolian Harp', *Kubla Khan*, *The Ancient Mariner*, or *Christabel* could not be blamed for dating these poems after Coleridge's rejection of mechanistic philosophy in 1801.

When this book is published, if I may indulge in a little prophecy, it will receive a British Library Cataloguing imprint which reads something like: '1. Coleridge, Samuel Taylor — Criticism and interpretation. 2. Science in literature. I. Title.' As such it will bridge, albeit inadequately and temporarily, the modern divide made famous in C. P. Snow's phrase, 'The Two Cultures'. In 1972, in a Friday-evening discourse at the Royal Institution titled 'Coleridge: A Bridge between Science and Poetry', Kathleen Coburn restated a fundamental truth for Coleridge scholarship: 'The view that Coleridge was anti-science is quite erroneous. Nor did he believe in a world of two cultures.' When in 1794 Coleridge began to use the public library in Bristol, Joseph Priestley's chemical discoveries were shelved next to his theological works. The historian of the Royal Society Thomas Birch was the editor of the works of the 'empiricist' Robert Boyle and also of the 'Neoplatonist' Ralph Cudworth. Today, in the deposit libraries of England Priestley's divergent studies are kept far apart; and one set of scholars studies the editions of Boyle, another studies the editions of Cudworth, and neither meet.

Coleridge scholarship has suffered from this cultural divide between the arts and the sciences. Because only scientists 'do' physics, we insist that Coleridge approach Newton as a scientist and judge him accordingly. Indeed, often we allow ourselves to do little more than probe Coleridge's complex thought about Newtonian science with such questions as 'Did Coleridge believe in the inverse-square law of gravitational attraction? Let's see now . . . yes or no?' If we find him writing approvingly of mechanistic science he is 'uncritical and naïve'; the moment he becomes critical he has 'rejected' the system and is having 'pretentions to original thought in science'.[23]

Yet Coleridge makes it quite clear from his writings that he is studying the natural philosophers for exactly the reasons that he is reading Milton or Shakespeare. He seeks from each the truths of those things that are important to him:

[23] Fruman, *Coleridge*, 131.

To MILTON's trump
The odorous groves of earth reparadis'd
Unbosom their glad echoes: inly hush'd
Adoring NEWTON his serener eye
Raises to heaven . . .
                    (*Religious Musings*, 379–83)

Here Milton and Newton are not separated by a cultural divide, but
have a unity of purpose in Coleridge's thought. It is a testament to
the prejudice against Newton's 'scientific' influence that some critics
have suggested that the Newton in the above passage is the Sir Isaac
Newton who wrote a commentary on Revelation. Such comments
merely replace the barriers that are demolished as we read the above
passage.

Indeed, even Coleridge's negative assessment of Newton five years
after writing *Religious Musings* indicates that he sees an essential
similarity in the activities of Newton and Milton. If it would take
the souls of 500 Newtons to make a Milton, the two must still have
been concerned with the same truths. Today we may be tempted to
say 'Oh, I think Yeats a hundred times greater than T. S. Eliot', but
few would attempt to compare Yeats with Rutherford, or Eliot with
J. J. Thomson.

In this book I wish to suggest that Coleridge's studies in the
1790s informed, crucially and deeply, the poetry that he wrote from
1795 onwards. Yet I am not concerned to reassert the mechanistic
school against Platonism or some other early philosophy. The
study is an attempt to build a bridge between the ancient and modern
influences on Coleridge and to show the continuity in ancient and
modern thought that existed at the end of the eighteenth century.
Moving between these different philosophies in the 1790s, Coleridge
developed a coherent picture of nature and society which crucially
informed his early significant poetry. The origins of this world-view
remained with him throughout his life.

The discussion opens with an investigation of Coleridge's understanding of the ancient tradition of knowledge, the myth of an
original body of wisdom that has passed through major civilizations
and cultures down to modern times. Believers in this 'hermetic'
tradition were able to demonstrate continuity between ancient and
modern thought, and Chapter 1 will show that Coleridge saw himself
as a part of this tradition. The second chapter will show that by
struggling to understand Newton's system of the world in the summer

of 1795 Coleridge achieved a sophisticated understanding of the metaphysical truths of the age. He believed these truths were preserved for his own age in the natural philosophers, the inheritors of the ancient tradition (Chapter 3).

Chapters 4 and 5 will then develop the argument that Coleridge saw the Newtonian philosophy of his day as the means of bringing about a revolution in contemporary society, preparing the way for the dawn of the millennial age that according to biblical chronology is soon to be upon us. The early vehicle for these ideas *Religious Musings* is the subject of a detailed reading in Chapter 6. In the final two chapters of the book the consequences of Coleridge's study of natural philosophy are examined for his thoughts on the life, imagination, and finally the poetry, of *The Ancient Mariner*.

1

The Ancient Tradition of Knowledge

> The stolen and perverted writings of Homer and Ovid, of Plato and Cicero, which all men ought to contemn, are set up by artifice against the sublime of the Bible. But when the new age is at leisure to pronounce, all will be set right, & these grand works of the more ancient, and consciously & professedly inspired men, will hold their proper rank, & the daughters of memory shall become the daughters of inspiration.
>
> Blake, Preface to *Milton*

WHEN Coleridge revised his epic poem *Religious Musings* for the second edition of his *Poems* in 1797, he added a new line which he then deleted from the text. Beneath the line he placed a Greek footnote which is still reproduced in modern editions of the poem. Here it is as it appears in the revision of the poem in Coleridge's hand. The poet is referring to Christ and the deleted line is italicized:

> Holy with Power
> He on the thought-benighted Sceptic beam'd
> Manifest Godhead, melting into day
> What Mists dim-floating of Idolatry
> Split and misshap'd the Omnipresent Sire:
> *Renewer of the ancient Truth!** And first
> By TERROR he uncharm'd the slumb'ring Spirit

> * Τὸ Νοητὸν δι‚ηοῆχασιν ἐις πολλῶν Θεῶν ἰδιότητας DAMAS. DE MYST. ÆGYPT.
> (BL MS Ashley 408, fol. 7)

In his formidable work on the origins of philosophy *The True Intellectual System of the Universe* written in Cambridge in the 1670s, the Platonist Ralph Cudworth had cited this passage of Greek, translating it as: 'Men have divided and multiplied the first Intelligible, or the one supreme Deity, into the properties of many Gods.'[1] However, the reference—'Damascius, *De Mysteriis Aegyptiorum*'

---

[1] *The True Intellectual System of the Universe: The First Part; Wherein, All the Reason and Philosophy Of Atheism is Confuted; and Its Impossibility Demonstrated* (1678), i. 461. Coleridge borrowed the work in the 2nd edn. by Thomas Birch, 2 vols. (1743); see *BLB* 55, 90. The 2nd edn. is used throughout.

(or, *Of the Egyptian Mysteries*) refers to a book which, as far as we know, the fourth-century philosopher Damascius the Syrian never wrote. I wish to begin this study by looking at the importance of this deleted line and its footnote for understanding the early thought and poetry of Coleridge.[2]

Ἀποφαίνεσθαί τε περὶ οὐσίας θεῶν καὶ γενέσεως, οὖς καὶ πῦρ εἶναι καὶ γῆν καὶ ὕδωρ. (Diog. Laer. Proem. n. 2)

[They teach their doctrine concerning the nature and origin of the gods, whom they think to be fire, earth and water.]

This is the concluding sentence of notes Coleridge wrote late in 1796 and titled 'Remarks &c on Atheism, some original, but most from Cudworth, Bayle, Brucker &c.'[3] Most of the notes, including the above passage, he took from Cudworth's *True Intellectual System*. The lines with which Coleridge ends his 'Remarks' are from *Lives of Eminent Philosophers* by the third-century biographer of the ancient philosophers Diogenes Laertius. Diogenes is discussing the origins of philosophy, generally believed in his day to have been barbaric, or non-Greek:

> The date of the Magians, beginning with Zoroaster the Persian, was 5,000 years before the fall of Troy . . . the Magi spend their time in the worship of the gods, in sacrifices and in prayers, implying that none but themselves have the ear of the gods. *They propound their views concerning the being and origin of the gods, whom they hold to be fire, earth, and water* [my emphasis]; they condemn the use of images, and especially the error of attributing to the divinities difference of sex. . . . Aristotle in the first book of his dialogue *On Philosophy* declares that the Magi are more ancient than the Egyptians . . . Clearchus of Soli in his tract *On Education* further makes the Gymnosophists to be descended from the Magi; and some trace the Jews also to the same origin. (i. prol., sects. 2–9; trans. R. D. Hicks, London, 1925)

Diogenes is relating the popular belief of his age that the ancient civilizations in Egypt and Persia were the originators of Greek philosophy. Fourteen hundred years later, Ralph Cudworth wrote *The True Intellectual System* also believing that there was a body of original knowledge given to man by revelation at the dawn of civilization, which had passed through the major cultures of the old

---

[2] John Beer is the only critic to have tackled the 'Damascius' footnote, and he concluded (in *Coleridge the Visionary*, 111) that it was probably a joke.

[3] BL MS Egerton 2801, fols. 212–15.

world until it entered and inspired the world of classical antiquity. This knowledge, known as the *prisca theologia* or *prisca sapientia*, was said to have influenced the Early Christian Fathers, and it re-emerged in the Renaissance with the discovery and translation of supposedly antique documents written by ancient theologians such as Zoroaster and Hermes Trismegistus. Coleridge borrowed *The True Intellectual System* in November 1796 and read it thoroughly enough to transcribe the two lines of Diogenes from the middle of a 450-page chapter. He too was interested in these beliefs, which are also called the 'ancient tradition of knowledge' or 'the Hermetic tradition'.[4]

By the middle of the second century AD the beliefs of Christianity had spread outside Palestine and had come up against the diverse religious cults and philosophies that flourished under the relative peace and tolerance of the Roman Empire. At this time a group of Hellenic Christians known as the Greek Apologists began to translate their Christian beliefs into the language of contemporary philosophy. Their intention was to give the new faith an intellectual respectability by showing its central position in the history and progress of mankind from the beginnings of civilization.[5] The Greek Apologists believed it was possible to translate the Judaeo-Christian writings and beliefs into the language of Greek metaphysics because there was an underlying similarity in the two cultures, explained by an original unity of ancient knowledge. The prophets of the Old Testament and the Greek philosophers had in their writings expressed faint ideas of eternal truths which were now fully revealed by Jesus Christ. To succeed in this mission the Early Church Fathers had to bring about a fundamental change in the attitude of contemporary pagan philosophers to writers such as Pythagoras, Plato, and Aristotle, who they believed had described eternal truths which merely required

---

[4] In an important article on the early influences on Coleridge ('Coleridge, Hartley, and the Mystics', *JHI* xx (1959), 477–94) Richard Haven asserted the influence of British empiricism on Coleridge in place of Neoplatonism. The fragmentary quotations from Cudworth in Coleridge's notes seem to confirm his view, which is shared by many scholars including Fruman, who asserts that 'some obscure jottings' are all Coleridge took from Cudworth (*Coleridge*, 475). But although the quotations are obscure, Coleridge also wrote a précis of the first 3 chapters of *True Intellectual System*.

[5] For the Greek Apologists see H. Chadwick, 'Philo and the Beginnings of Christian Philosophy', in A. H. Armstrong (ed.), *The Cambridge History of Later Greek and Early Medieval Philosophy* (Cambridge, 1967), 133–92.

commentary.[6] The Greek Apologists argued that although the writings of the earlier philosophers showed fragments of the religious truths of monotheism, Trinitarianism, etc., these were none the less poorly conceived, and clouded by mistakes and wild guesses such as the transmigration of souls. Everything that was true in Greek philosophy was to be found more clearly expressed, though often in myth, in the early books of the Bible. Hence through biblical commentaries they attempted to show that the writings of Moses in the Pentateuch and the works of the early philosophers were fundamentally alike. Yet as it could be shown that the Pentateuch was both older and truer than the most ancient Greek writings, they claimed that the Bible was the source of all other philosophies. Either the Greeks had stolen their ideas, or the descendants of Moses had taught the Greeks. These ideas have lasted: 'The stolen and perverted writings of Homer and Ovid, of Plato and Cicero, which all men ought to contemn', wrote William Blake in 1800, 'are set up by artifice against the sublime of the Bible.'

The early Christians thus argued that as the Pentateuch was older, it was closer to an original revelation of God to man in an antediluvian golden age. The biblical story of the Fall of Man supported this, as did Plato's *Timaeus* and *Critias* which propound the notion of a past age of clarity and truth which subsequent peoples had corrupted.[7]

The Christian Fathers believed that the 'ancient knowledge' was to be found in supposedly very ancient texts, the Hermetica, Orphica, Sibylline Prophecies, and the Pythagorean *Carmina Aurea* which were composed by the ancient prophets and theologians Hermes Trismegistus, Orpheus, the Sibyls, and Zoroaster.[8] The ancient authors, it was thought, were the founders of the different national religious traditions, as Moses had been for the Jews: Zoroaster was linked with the faith of the Chaldeans and Persians, Hermes with the Egyptians, and Orpheus with the Greeks. Although written many centuries before Christ, the texts seemed to anticipate the truths of

---

[6] In fact, the syncretist tendencies of the Neopythagorean and Neoplatonic systems bear little resemblance to their founders; see R. T. Wallis, *Neo-platonism* (London, 1972), 123–33.

[7] The myth of Atlantis is usefully discussed by Lee in his Appendix to Plato, *Timaeus and Critias*, trans. D. Lee (London, 1971), 146–67.

[8] See D. P. Walker, *The Ancient Theology: Studies in Christian Platonism from the Fifteenth to the Eighteenth Century* (London, 1972), 1–41.

Christianity. Hence, in order to preserve the uniqueness of the Judaeo-Christian tradition, it was usual to claim that the pagan theologians had stolen their ideas from the ancestors of Moses who had taught at Sidon.

The Early Church Fathers also used certain passages in the New Testament to support their thesis: the sower casting seed on fertile and sterile ground[9] became a parable of the seeds of the *logos*, partial manifestations of the Word of God to the prophets of the Old Testament and to inspired men in other cultures, some of whom had understood and preserved these truths. Equally important was the Epistle to the Romans, where St Paul wrote in condemnation of the Greeks: 'That which may be known of God is manifest in them; for God hath shewed it unto them. For the invisible things of him from the creation of the world are clearly seen, being understood by the things that are made, even his eternal power and Godhead; so that they are without excuse'.[10] Although Paul is berating the Greeks for not reading the 'book of Nature', it was possible to read Romans to mean that some pagan philosophers should be admitted because they had correctly interpreted God's natural language.

The writings of the ancient theologians were thus explained either as pre-Christian revelations of the *logos* (like those given to the Jewish Patriarchs); or as borrowings from the revealed truths of the Pentateuch. Although the loan theory was more popular, a problem for the Apologists was that some of these 'ancient' writings contain more Christian theology than could be found in the Old Testament. As the texts of the ancient theologians are generally post-Christian fakes from the first four centuries after Christ, this is not very surprising, but it was to have an important effect when the tradition, then known as Hermeticism, re-emerged in the Renaissance:[11] for when in the fifteenth century Plato began to be studied once more, the works of the ancient theologians were also revived.[12]

By now, however, the original reason for an appeal to ancient sources had disappeared: Christianity was the dominant religion of

---

[9] Matt. 13: 3-9.   [10] 1: 19-20

[11] A.-J. Festugière, the greatest modern authority on the ancient texts, considers that they are mainly Greek, a Hellenistic amalgam of Platonism, Stoicism, Judaism, and Christianity, set in a Gnostic and magical framework; see *La Révélation d'Hermès Trismégiste*, 3rd edn., i (Paris, 1950), 1-80.

[12] The classic study of Renaissance Hermeticism is F. A. Yates, *Giordano Bruno and the Hermetic Tradition* (London, 1964).

the western world and there were no pagan philosophers left to convert. Thus Hermeticism soon became a potential rival to the Judaeo-Christian tradition. Instead of remaining subordinate to Moses and the Patriarchs, the ancient theologians could be considered to have preserved the ancient wisdom more faithfully than either Jew or Greek. Less orthodox Hermeticists like Giordano Bruno argued that the corpus of writings clearly contained religious insights not evident in the Mosaic account, and so subordinated Christianity, the younger faith, to the ancient tradition, representing Christ as a member of the preaching band of theologians who originated with Zoroaster and Hermes and stretched down the ages. Hence Bruno inverted the *prisca theologia*, making it the authentic tradition of which Christianity was not the summation, but merely another manifestation. This exploited the contradiction in the tradition: for if men were in a state of complete knowledge at the beginning of the world there could be no genuine progress. Christianity was the restoration of authentic knowledge, and Christ, as Coleridge put it in *Religious Musings*, merely the 'Renewer of the Ancient Truth!'

In 1614, fourteen years after Bruno was burnt at the stake by the Inquisition for his work, Isaac Casaubon published *De rebus sacris et ecclesiasticis exercitationes* at the court of James I; he exposed the myth of the ancient tradition as a Christian fabrication perpetrated during the first centuries AD. Yet this shattering of the ancient tradition was evaded for many years, as later writers needed the supposedly ancient texts to check the truth of the new mechanical philosophies of the age.

Two important Neoplatonic writers who defended the ancient tradition in the seventeenth century were Henry More and Ralph Cudworth, who wrote and taught at Cambridge.[13] Both men saw it their task to evaluate the new philosophies of Hobbes, Descartes, and Spinoza and to measure them against the philosophy of the ancient knowledge. In *Conjectura Cabbalistica. Or, A Conjectural Essay of Interpreting the Minde of Moses, according to a Threefold Cabbala*[14] More demonstrated his 'pedigree' method for Descartes:

---

[13] For the background to the Platonic revival in England see E. Cassirer, *The Platonic Renaissance in England*, trans. J. P. Pettegrove (Edinburgh, 1953); B. Willey, *The Seventeenth-Century Background: Studies in the Thought of the Age in Relation to Poetry and Religion* (London, 1934), 123–54.

[14] Published in *A Collection of Several Philosophical Writings of Dr. Henry More*, 4th edn. (1712–13).

Wherefore the *Cartesian* Philosophy being in a manner the same with that of *Democritus*, and that of *Democritus* the same with the Physiological part of *Pythagoras* his Philosophy; and *Pythagoras* his Philosophy, the same with the *Sidonian*; as also the *Sidonian* with the *Mosaical*; it will necessarily follow, that the *Mosaical* Philosophy, in the Physiological part thereof, is the same with the *Cartesian*. (p. 114)

The most elaborate and thorough comparison of the ancient, authentic body of knowledge with the modern systems was Cudworth's 900-page *The True Intellectual System*, which actually served generations as the principal source of Greek philosophy. This opens with a description of the atomistic philosophy of the Greeks Leucippus and Democritus, which Cudworth, following the work of Johann Arcerius the Friesian philologist and the Commonwealth antiquary John Selden, believed was a corruption of a more ancient system, traceable through the Pythagoreans to Moses' descendants at Sidon. Hence Cudworth argued that far from leading to atheism, the atomistic philosophy was divinely revealed in ancient times. As it must also be reconcilable with Christianity, a modern statement with atheistic conclusions, such as that of Thomas Hobbes, was obviously wrong.

Coleridge borrowed *The True Intellectual System* for two and a half weeks in May 1795 to write his Bristol lectures on religion, and again in November 1796, for a month. It is probably on the second reading that he wrote the 'Remarks, &c. on Atheism'. This is how they begin:

The division of Primary & secondary Qualities — or the making heat, color &c, *caused* by the external, but inhering only in the sentient, first held by Moschus, or Mochus, a Phoenician, who according to Strabo, lived before the Trojan War — and who is supposed by Arcerius whose conjecture is approved by Selden, to have been Moses: this Philosophy was afterwards adopted by Leucippus, and shortly after by Democritus, who was born the year after Socrates. (BL MS Egerton 2801, fol. 212)

The lines are taken directly from the first chapter of *The True Intellectual System*:

the first inventor of this atomical philosophy was one *Moschus* a *Phoenician*, who, as *Strabo* also notes, lived before the *Trojan* Wars. . . . Mr *Selden* approves of the conjecture of *Arcerius*, the publisher of *Jamblichus*, that this *Mochus* was no other than the celebrated *Moses* of the *Jews*, with whose successors the Jewish philosophers, priests and prophets, *Pythagoras* conversed at *Sidon*. (i. 12–13)

Cudworth's views on atomism were extreme even for the seventeenth century, as most adherents of the ancient tradition were content to trace an intellectual pedigree for atomism in the Pythagorean theory of monads, thence to the philosophers in Egypt and Phoenicia, where Pythagoras was thought to have studied, and so to Genesis.[15] George Berkeley noted this more moderate tradition seventy years later in his Neoplatonic essay *Siris*:[16]

> There are traces of profound thought as well as primeval tradition in the Platonic, Pythagorean, Ægyptian, and Chaldaic philosophy. Men in those early days were not over laid with languages and literature. Their minds seem to have been more exercised, and less burdened, than in later ages; and, as so much nearer the beginning of the world, to have had the advantage of patriarchal lights handed down through a few hands. It cannot indeed be affirmed (how probable soever it may seem) that Moses was that same Mochus, with whose successors, priests and prophets, Pythagoras is said to have conversed at Sidon. (*Works of George Berkeley*, ii. 598)

Endorsing Cudworth, Coleridge had adopted views which were, even two generations before, anachronistic and unsubstantiated. In the eighteenth century the prevalent view was that Moses had 'reached the summit of human learning' and had become 'a perfect master of astronomy, geometry, music, medicine, occult philosophy, and, in short, of the whole circle of the arts and sciences which were at that time known'.[17] His wisdom was supposed to have been learnt from the ancient Egyptians, and then transmitted through the oral Jewish *cabbala* and through lost scriptures known to Pythagoras and Plato. Many writers were sceptical about these claims and attributed them to Hellenizing Jewish scholars at the time of Christ, but in his second lecture on revealed religion Coleridge noted: 'Moses is said to have been learned in all the learning of the Ægyptians.'[18]

---

[15] See D. B. Sailor, 'Moses and Atomism', *JHL* xxv (1964), 3–16; reprinted in C. A. Russell (ed.), *Science and Religious Belief* (London, 1973), 5–19.

[16] *Siris: a Chain of Philosophical Reflections and Inquiries Concerning the Virtues of Tarwater, And divers other Subjects connected together and arising one from another* (1744), in *The Works of George Berkeley, DD Late Bishop of Cloyne in Ireland*, 2 vols. (1784). Coleridge borrowed *Siris* in March 1796 (*BLB* 75) the latter sections of which are taken up with the *prisca sapientia*.

[17] William Enfield, *The History of Philosophy, from the earliest times to the beginning of the present century, drawn up from Brücker's* Historia Critica Philosophiae, 2 vols. (1791), i. 19–20. Coleridge borrowed vol. i of this work in March–April 1795 (*BLB*[43).

[18] *Lectures 1795*, 135.

The most obvious problem about linking the Bible to atomistic philosophies ancient or modern is, of course, that the Bible does not mention any. The account of the Creation in Genesis cannot support mechanical philosophy. Thomas Paine pointed to this obvious fact in his irreverent and entertaining appraisal of the biblical canon *The Age of Reason*:[19]

> Why it has been called the Mosaic account of the creation, I am at a loss to conceive. Moses, I believe, was too good a judge of such subjects to put his name to that account. He had been educated among the Egyptians, who were a people as well skilled in science, and particularly in astronomy, as any people of their day; and the silence and caution that Moses observes, in not authenticating the account, is a good negative evidence that he neither told it, nor believed it. (p. 15)

Paine's argument is interesting for one who is usually portrayed as an entirely negative critic of the Bible. Rather than arguing that as Genesis is incoherent, Moses must have been an idiot (his usual line on the prophets), he suggests that Moses understood the Egyptian wisdom and the true account of creation too well to have written it. Coleridge must also have been aware that Genesis is not a complex metaphysical analysis of God's causal action in the world, and thus gives no direct support for the origins of atomism in the ancient tradition. Yet the belief that there were books written by Moses that had then been lost was part of the Hermeticist's folklore.

Isaac Newton was only one of several Old Testament scholars who believed that Genesis is a potted version of several books about the world before the Flood. 'The Pentateuch', Newton wrote, 'is composed of the law and the history of God's people together; and the history hath been collected from several books: such as were the History of the Creation composed by Moses, Gen. ii. 4; the Book of the Generations of Adam, Gen. v. [1]; and the Book of the Wars of the Lord, Num. xxi. 14.'[20] As Coleridge knew Newton's Old Testament work,[21] he would have had no difficulty explaining why

---

[19] *The Age of Reason: Being An Investigation of True and of Fabulous Theology*, part 1 (1793), 2nd edn. (1795).

[20] *Observations Upon the Prophecies of Holy Writ, particularly the Prophecies of Daniel, and the Apocalypse of St. John*, in *Isaaci Newtoni Opera Quae Exstant Omnia*, ed. Samuel Horsley, 5 vols. (1779–85) v. 299.

[21] 'Sir I. Newton observes in P309 of his "Prophecies of holy Writ", Horsley's Edition, that Ruler is signified by his riding on a beast—justly—for none but beasts need have rulers' (*CN* i. 83).

the account in Genesis contained none of the knowledge that he imputed to Moses.

Thus while Paine took the absence of natural theology in the Bible to discount the authenticity of the text, Coleridge was willing to trace the origins of knowledge to the Pentateuch, not because he could read it there, but because, as the oldest record of man, it must be preserving the original revelation. Hence he can be charged with holding a belief which is unprovable in arguing that the wisdom of later nations is to be taken as evidence of an original and brighter wisdom in their predecessors, in whose writings no trace of this is to be found.

The fourth and longest chapter of *The True Intellectual System* reviews the thought of all the philosophers of the ancient tradition, discussing the work of Zoroaster, Orpheus, Hermes, the classical poets, the pre-Socratic philosophers Pythagoras and Heraclitus, and Socrates, Plato, and Aristotle. Cudworth intended to prove in the chapter that all the philosophers of the true tradition had an idea of the Christian doctrines of the one Supreme God and of the Trinity. In the frontispiece of the book he had portrayed Pythagoras, Socrates, and Aristotle on one side of a classical portico beneath a laurel wreath and a plaque inscribed 'Theists'; and opposing them the 'Atheists' Anaximander, Strato, and Epicurus, beneath a broken wreath. Cudworth defined an atheist as one who denies that there is 'one perfect living and understanding being . . . the original of all things, and the architect of the whole universe'.[22] Yet it is only by the most elaborate exegesis that he is able to convince his reader that the philosophers he supports are theists: a difficulty which actually accounts for the colossal length of his chapter. An interesting example of this rather specious method is the pre-Socratic philosopher Heraclitus, who developed a monist theory in which the principle of all things was a fiery substantial nature called *logos*.[23] Heraclitus is only reconciled with traditional theism at the risk of violating his original conception of the universe, yet Cudworth cast him among the theists because Heraclitus was a disciple of Empedocles, who, as he was taught by Pythagoras, must have been part of the ancient tradition from the original Mosaic revelation.

[22] *True Intellectual System*, i. 106.
[23] See J. Barnes, *The PreSocratic Philosophers*, 2 vols. (London, 1979), i. 57–81; W. K. C. Guthrie, 'The Early PreSocratics and the Pythagoreans', in id. (ed.), *A History of Greek Philosophy*, i (Cambridge, 1962), 403–92.

Once Coleridge is understood to be endorsing the account of the ancient tradition which he had read in Cudworth, several of his more obscure pronouncements and references begin to make sense. Consider these statements on Plato from the 1795 lectures on religion:

> Plato, the wild-minded Disciple of Socrates who hid Truth in a dazzle of fantastic allegory, and is dark with excess of Brightness . . . (*Lectures 1795*, 208)

> But though Plato dressed Truth in the garb of Nonsense, still it was Truth, and they who would take the Trouble of unveiling her, might discover and distinguish all the Features . . . (ibid. 209)

Plato's philosophy contains truth because it was passed down to him by Socrates who in turn received it from the philosophers of the ancient tradition. Plato is thus a member of this tradition, even if his writings are perverse renderings of the original revelation. In the tradition of ancient knowledge it was quite common to talk about the perversion and adulteration of original truths. The further from the original, the more adulterated were the texts. Thus Christ had to become the '*Renewer* of the ancient Truth' (my emphasis), because by his time the original revelation had become buried over the many preceding centuries in the myths and interpretations of several different cultures.

In *Religious Musings*, the poem which occupied Coleridge erratically between December 1794 and March 1796, the ancient tradition of philosophers is present as an 'elect band' of past and present statesmen, philosophers, and poets who have received and preserved ancient Truths and whose number Coleridge aspired to join:

> whoe'er from earliest time
> With conscious zeal had urged Love's wondrous plan
> Coadjutors of God . . .   (377–9)

Milton, Newton, Hartley, Franklin, and Priestley are celebrated as members of this tradition in the published version, but the reference to those who from 'earliest time' have urged the 'wondrous plan' suggests that the poet had other philosophers in mind. Deleted lines from this section of the manuscript bear this out:

> There to PLATO's gaze
> Sweep brighter Visions than on elder days

> He of ancient days
> Wisest, nor haply uninspir'd of God
> Mild Socrates.

(Variants from 'Rugby MS', fols. 56, 58)

The Socratic school, condemned by the poet for perverting truth, had itself been perverted by later philosophies: 'The simple Doctrines of the pure Socratic School', he wrote, 'had yielded to the Stoic and Epicurean.'[24]

Coleridge pursued the idea of corruption from a golden age in his final lecture on religion. In the fragmentary 'Fable of the maddening rain' he relates how one just man escapes the rain-storm which transforms the age of virtue into the age of corruption. Despairing as the only one with sanity after the rain, the prophet soaks himself in the water and becomes the leader. Coleridge told the story as an allegory of the careers of Pitt and Burke who deserted the reforming cause in the 1790s for political power. But the fable was more widely applicable, describing the perversion of an original state by those entrusted by God to preserve it.

Yet unlike the politicians, the ancient theologians had not entirely destroyed the original truths. Indeed they retained enough integrity for Coleridge to aspire to join their ranks:

> And blest are they,
> Who in this fleshly World, the elect of Heaven,
> Their strong eye darting thro' the deeds of Men
> Adore with stedfast unpresuming gaze
> Him, Nature's Essence, Mind, and Energy!

(*Religious Musings*, 51–5)

> Holies of God!
> (And what if Monads of the infinite mind?)
> I haply journeying my immortal course
> Shall sometime join your mystic choir!

(Ibid. 425–8)

Yet what was this precious original revelation which Christ came to restore? What exactly had God revealed to Moses, which had then become so garbled and perverted by his descendants, the ancient theologians? Coleridge's answer to this in 1796 betrays his own beliefs: the ancient revealed truth was the Unitarian knowledge of

---

[24] *Lectures 1795*, 156.

the one supreme God, for it was this which the Unitarians believed
had been replaced by the later and corrupted doctrine of the Trinity.
Thus, when in 1797 he contemplated the revision of *Religious
Musings* he linked Unitarianism and the ancient tradition:

> Holy with Power
> He on the thought-benighted Sceptic beam'd
> Manifest Godhead, melting into day
> What Mists dim-floating of Idolatry
> Split and misshap'd the Omnipresent Sire:
> Renewer of the ancient Truth!* And first
> By TERROR he uncharm'd the slumb'ring Spirit.

* [*Greek text for:* Men have divided and multiplied the first Intelligible, or the one
Supreme Deity, into the properties of many Gods.] DAMAS. DE MYST. ÆGYPT.
(BL MS Ashley 408, fol. 7)

In the context of the revision, the 'Damas.' footnote makes perfectly
good sense. Christ is to renew 'the ancient Truth' of 'the one supreme
Deity' (Unitarianism) which has become corrupted by the successors
of Moses, particularly the Greek philosophers, into a doctrine of
'many Gods' (Trinitarianism). Once again Cudworth is the source
of the footnote, which is quoted in *The True Intellectual System* to
show that the Egyptians had once worshipped one supreme God.[25]
The passage was written by Damascius the Syrian, a fourth-century
pagan Neoplatonist, who composed a commentary on the principal
source of Egyptian philosophy, a third-century work called *Of the
Egyptian Mysteries* by Iamblichus.[26] The footnote suited the argument in *Religious Musings* that the elect band understand the truth
of the one God even though others have split the deity into a trinity
of Gods. Coleridge thus added in the poem: 'For THEY dare know
of what may seem deform / The SUPREME FAIR sole Operant.'[27]

[25] Cudworth gave the reference to this passage, which occurs at i. 461, as
'Damasc. de Princ. M.S.', and Birch added '[Vide Wolfii Anecdota Graeca, Tom. III.
p. 260]'. Wolf's collection of Greek manuscripts contained selections from Damascius,
Dubitationes et solutiones de primis principiis, first published complete in *Damascii
philosophi Platonici Quaestiones de primis principiis*, ed. C. A. Ruelle, 2 vols. (1889).
Damascius' work is a commentary on Plato's *Parmenides*, and attacks Plotinus and
supports Iamblichus.
[26] Thomas Gale published an edition of *De Mysteriis Ægyptiorum* in 1678 with
end-notes by Damascius, and Birch used this work in editing ch. 4 sect. 18 of *True
Intellectual System*. This probably explains why Coleridge conflated Damascius and
Egyptian Mysteries in his reference, which would correctly read 'Damas. de Primis
Princ.'   [27] ll. 61–2.

In September 1796 Coleridge borrowed from the Bristol Library *The Philosophical Principles of Natural and Revealed Religion*[28] by Andrew Ramsay, a friend of Hume and Fénelon and a strong defender of the ancient tradition of knowledge. In this work Ramsay discussed the need for a band of philosophers to carry forward the ancient symbols that Christ had restored. When Ramsay looked for ancient truths in his own age, he had no doubt that the natural philosophy of Sir Isaac Newton was an uncorrupted restatement of ancient knowledge, and Ramsay added Newton's name to the list of ancient theologians. There are strong indications that Newton would have accepted Ramsay's assessment. Drafting the second book of *Principia Mathematica*, Newton had written:

It was the most ancient opinion of those who applied themselves to Philosophy, that the fixed stars stood immovable in the highest parts of the world, that under them the planets revolved about the sun, that the earth, as one of the planets, described an annual course about the sun, while by a diurnal motion it turned on its axis, and that the sun remained at rest in the center of the universe. . . . The Egyptians were the earliest observers of the heavens, and from them, probably, this philosophy spread abroad. For from them it was, and from the nations about them, that the Greeks, a people more addicted to the study of philology than of Nature, derived their first, as well as their soundest, notions of philosophy . . . (CUL Add. MS 3990, fol. 1)

Coleridge too believed that Newton was one of the elect band: 'inly hush'd / Adoring NEWTON his serener eye / Raises to heaven', he wrote in *Religious Musings*.[29] Yet Coleridge also thought that the tradition was soon to end, for the world was drawing towards the seventh and final millennium. If the God-given wisdom had been preserved and restored for any reason, it was now that this would be revealed. Thus two of the last members of the ancient tradition were the philosophers David Hartley and Joseph Priestley who had begun the task of applying the fundamental truths of Newton's natural philosophy to the moral world:

> inly hush'd
> Adoring NEWTON his serener eye
> Raises to heaven: and he of mortal kind
> Wisest, he* first who mark'd the ideal tribes
> Down the fine fibres from the sentient brain
> Roll subtly-surging. Pressing on his steps

---

[28] 2 vols. (1748–9)   [29] ll. 381–3.

> Lo! Priestley there, Patriot, and Saint, and Sage,
> Whom that my fleshly eye hath never seen . . .
>
> *DAVID HARTLEY.
>
> (Religious Musings, 381–8)

The introduction of the poet himself at this moment is quite purposeful, for Coleridge believed that he was the next, perhaps the last, elect being to disseminate truth before the millennium. Although a novice, he declares at the end of the poem: 'I haply journeying my immortal course / Shall sometime join your mystic choir!'[30]

In a farewell address to his Dissenting congregation at Hackney in April 1794, Priestley took as his theme the signs that would warn mankind of the approaching millennium.[31] Reminding his listeners that Christ had told men to be 'on the watch' for the new age, Priestley described the moral and natural upheavals that were to occur in the final epoch of the world. 'Watch therefore, for you know neither the day nor the hour' is the warning at the end of Christ's parable of the Wise and Foolish Virgins. Coleridge took note of this in the millennial motto of *The Watchman*, his 1796 journal:

> That All may know the TRUTH;
> And that the TRUTH may make us FREE!!
>
> (The Watchman, 3)

Behind the young poet was an auspicious tradition of those who had preserved an ancient knowledge. In *Religious Musings* Socrates, Plato, Christ and the disciples, the Neoplatonists, Milton, Newton, Berkeley, Hartley, Franklin, and Priestley are all present in celebration of this tradition. Next to come was the young prophet of the fast-approaching millennium, whose knowledge and visionary power were yet to be spread throughout the land.

---

[30] ll. 427–9.

[31] Joseph Priestley, *The present State of Europe compared with Antient Prophecies; A Sermon, preached at The Gravel Pit Meeting in Hackney, February 28, 1794, Being the Day appointed for a General Fast*. Priestley took his text from Matt. 3: 2: 'Repent ye; for the kingdom of heaven is at hand.'

2
Wrestling with the Spirit of Newton

There, Priest of Nature! dost thou shine,
NEWTON! a King among the Kings divine.

Coleridge, 'A Greek Ode on Astronomy', trans. Southey

It has been asserted that Sir Isaac Newton's philosophy leads
in its consequences to Atheism: perhaps not without reason.

Coleridge, *Joan of Arc*, book II

IN 1795, at the age of 22, Samuel Taylor Coleridge began to write
some of the most speculative and philosophical poetry of the modern
age. In little over a year, in just three poems, 'The Eolian Harp',
Joan of Arc book II, and *Religious Musings*, he drew on philosophies
and themes from several centuries of thought to express the religious
and metaphysical beliefs which later became the sophisticated
philosophical system of his life's work.[1] In this chapter I will
develop the argument that it was his struggle to accept the modern
system of the world of Isaac Newton that caused the extraordinary
burst of complex poetry in these months.

By 1727, the year of Newton's death, almost everyone had
accepted the mathematical system of the world which Newton had
described some forty years earlier in *Philosophiae Naturalis Principia
Mathematica*. The universe became a self-sustaining system of
matter in motion, governed by simple laws which were everywhere
applicable and which man could discern and apply. The simple force
of gravity acted to move material objects, whether these be planets
circling distant stars, or apples falling from trees. There was an
overwhelming economy and simplicity to nature and the unchanging
laws that governed her operations.

Few people would have dissented from this summary of Newton's
system of the world in 1727. One of them, unfortunately, would
have been Newton:

It is inconceivable, that inanimate brute matter should, without the mediation
of something else, which is not material, operate upon and affect other matter

---

[1] For an authoritative account of the influence of natural philosophy on Coleridge's
later thought see Levere, *Poetry Realized in Nature*.

without mutual contact; as it must do, if gravitation, in the sense of *Epicurus*, be essential and inherent in it. And this is one reason, why I desired you would not ascribe innate gravity to me. That gravity should be innate, inherent and essential to matter, so that one body may act upon another at a distance through a *vacuum*, without the mediation of any thing else, by and through which their action and force may be conveyed from one to another, is to me so great an absurdity, that I believe no man who has in philosophical matters a competent faculty of thinking, can ever fall into it. Gravity must be caused by an agent acting constantly according to certain laws; but whether this agent be material or immaterial, I have left to the consideration of my readers. (letter to Bentley, 25 February 1692/3; *Opera*, ed. Horsley, iv. 438)

Newton ended his long life revising his biblical scholarship, and believing that Nature had actually yielded very few of her secrets to him. He catalogued the questions he would like to have been able to answer in the thirty-five 'Queries' that he added in 1717 to the second edition of the *Opticks*. The genius of these alone kept philosophers occupied until the early part of this century: '*Quest. 30.* Are not gross Bodies and Light convertible into one another?' Newton, however, believed that there were many more questions he had not even thought of:

I don't know what I may seem to the world, but, as to myself, I seem to have been only like a boy playing on the sea shore, and diverting myself in now and then finding a smoother pebble or a prettier shell than ordinary, whilst the great ocean of truth lay all undiscovered before me. (Anecdote attributed to Andrew Ramsay; quoted in Westfall, *Newton at Rest*, 863)

In his chief works, the *Philosophiae Naturalis Principia Mathematica* of 1687 and the *Opticks, Or A Treatise on the Reflections, Refractions, Inflections and Colours of Light* of 1704, Newton gave descriptive accounts of the observed phenomena of the motions of bodies and the behaviour of light. But he also had wished to give a *causal* account of the universe, by demonstrating those springs of motion that were not observable by the senses. In the 1660s as a young man at Cambridge, Newton had read the 'moderns' Descartes and Spinoza when he should have been reading Aristotle, and he had also met those keepers of the ancient tradition, the Cambridge Platonists Ralph Cudworth and Henry More.

When Newton met the latter they were at the height of their powers and had rejected Cartesian dualism for the Platonic hierarchy of being. Identifying what More called 'the spirit of Nature' and Cudworth 'the plastick life of nature', the Platonists had conceived the cause of motion in the world to act from within nature itself, a principle that was, in turn, responsive only to the command and will of the deity. Hence they conceived of a hierarchy of being throughout nature: the 'great chain of Being' as it became known.[2] John Locke described this in *An Essay Concerning Human Understanding* (1690):

finding in all parts of the Creation, that fall under humane Observation, that there is a gradual connexion of one with another, without any great or discoverable gaps between, in all that great variety of Things we see in the World, which are so closely linked together, that, in the several ranks of Beings, it is not easy to discover the bounds betwixt them, we have reason to be perswaded, that by such gentle steps Things ascend upwards in degrees of Perfection. (bk. IV, ch. 16, sect. 12)

Newton received inscribed books from Henry More and his notes from Cudworth's *The True Intellectual System* have survived.[3] From these early influences Newton was prompted to consider whether force and activity in the world could be explained by some intermediary agent, such as a world soul, or a plastic spirit, or whether, as Descartes believed, they were the direct and constant expression of divine action. For a while he rejected the Platonists' ideas of intermediates. However, in the 1670s his alchemical studies overwhelmed him with the sheer diversity of activity within materials, which heated up, changed colour, exploded, expanded, shone, liquefied, fermented, and exhaled gases. These results began to suggest to him the existence of powerful agents within nature, and Newton now considered whether there was an agent of divine action which transmitted God's energy into each part of nature. He called his hypothetical agent 'aether' after the 'aer' of the pre-Socratic metaphysicians. By 1675 Newton was beginning to speculate how aether might act:

---

[2] For the plenitude of nature see A. O. Lovejoy, *The Great Chain of Being: A Study of the History of an Idea* (Cambridge, Mass., 1936).

[3] Newton's undergraduate notebook of 1661–5 indicates a close reading of Henry More's *Immortality of the Soul*, one of the seven volumes by More in his library, two of which were inscribed by their author: see G. A. J. Rogers, 'Locke, Newton, and the Cambridge Platonists on Innate Ideas', *JHI* xl (1979), 195–8; J. Harrison, *The Library of Isaac Newton* (Cambridge, 1978), 195–6. Newton also made 4 folio pages of notes from *True Intellectual System*: see J. E. McGuire, 'Force, Active Principles, and Newton's Invisible Realm'. *Ambix*, xv (1968), 204.

for nature is a perpetual worker, generating fluids out of solids, and solids out of fluids, fixed things out of volatile, and volatile out of fixed, subtil out of gross and gross out of subtil; some things to ascend, and make the upper terrestrial juices, rivers, and the atmosphere; and by consequence, others to descend for a requital to the former. And, as the earth, so perhaps may the sun imbibe this spirit copiously, to conserve his shining, and keep the planets from receding further from him. And they, that will, may also suppose, that this spirit affords or carries with it thither the solary fewel and material principle of light: and that the vast aethereal spaces between us and the stars are for a sufficient repository for this food of the sun and planets.

Although Newton sent these thoughts in a letter to Henry Oldenburg, he was unwilling for them to be published and they remained in manuscript until 1757.[4] Newton was aware that aether could be interpreted as an independent principle of activity in the world, and that his system thus flirted with deism. Thus he qualified his views:

the frame of nature may be nothing but aether condensed by a fermental principle . . . may be nothing but various contextures of some certain aetherial spirits or vapours condensed, as it were, by precipitation, much after the manner, that vapours . . . wrought into various forms, at first by the immediate hand of the Creator, and ever since by the power of nature, who by virtue of the command, *Increase and multiply*, became a complete imitator of the copies set her by the Protoplast. Thus perhaps may all things be originated from aether . . . (letter of 7 December 1695; *The Works of the Honourable Robert Boyle*, ed. Thomas Birch, 2nd edn., 6 vols. (1772), i, p. cxviii)[5]

This is Platonism: the order of nature is maintained by aether, and the phenomena generated are physical copies of divine Ideas. The problem for the empirical philosopher was that it was also speculation: Newton could get no direct proof of the existence of aether. He dare not publish such ideas.

In *Principia* the aether hypothesis received a short paragraph at the very end of the treatise:

---

[4] Thomas Birch, editor of Cudworth's *True Intellectual System*, published Newton's letter in *The History of the Royal Society of London, for improving of Natural Knowledge, from its first rise*, iii (1757), 251.

[5] The full text of the letter is in *The Correspondence of Isaac Newton*, ed. H. W. Turnbull, i (Cambridge, 1959), 362–86.

And now we might add something concerning a certain most subtle spirit which pervades and lies hid in all gross bodies; by the force and action of which spirit the particles of bodies attract one another at near distances, and cohere, if contiguous; and electric bodies operate to greater distances, as well repelling as attracting the neighbouring corpuscles; and light is emitted, reflected, refracted, inflected, and heats bodies; and all sensation is excited, and the members of animal bodies move at the command of the will, namely, by the vibrations of this spirit, mutually propagated along the solid filaments of the nerves, from the outward organs of sense to the brain, and from the brain into the muscles. But these are things that cannot be explained in a few words, nor are we furnished with that sufficiency of experiments which is required to an accurate determination and demonstration of the laws by which this electric and elastic spirit operates. (bk. III, General Scholium; trans. Andrew Motte, *Sir Isaac Newton's Mathematical Principles of Natural Philosophy and his System of the World* (1729), rev. F. Cajori (Berkeley, Calif., 1934), 547)

It is a haunting note on which to end the work, for it was another 30 years before Newton returned in print to the question of causation.

In 1717, revising the *Opticks* of 1704, Newton added the 'Queries' and suggested that the cause of gravity was a 'rare, subtile and elastick' medium called aether which expanded through the tracts of space between planetary bodies and impelled them towards each other. Perhaps, he thought, all forces in nature—electricity and magnetism, heat and light—might be transmitted by this material fluid which, composed of particles many times smaller than atoms, possessed a large repulsive force to propel matter through space.[6]

Newton lived with two world-views. As an empiricist he was concerned to describe how the world appeared, not to speculate on its inner workings. As a Platonist he wished to describe the entire system. Aether was the link between these two philosophies, the *arche* between the worlds of matter and spirit. At the top of the hierarchy of matter, it controlled matter, but was directed by higher causal principles that would not yield to man's investigations.[7]

---

[6] The clearest contemporary description of aether is in P. M. Heimann and J. E. McGuire, 'Newtonian Forces and Lockean Powers: Concepts of Matter in Eighteenth-Century Thought', *Historical Studies in the Physical Sciences*, iii (1971), 242–3. See also G. N. Cantor and M. J. S. Hodge (eds.), *Conceptions of Ether: Studies in the History of Ether Theories 1740–1900*, (Cambridge, 1981), 19–24.

[7] 'The Philosophy which Mr. *Newton* in his *Principles* and *Optiques* has pursued is Experimental; and it is not the business of Experimental Philosophy to teach the Causes of things any further than they can be proved by Experiments' ('An Account

The world-view changed. Cartesian dualism replaced the Neo-platonic hierarchies of being. Newtonian empiricism became the supreme philosophical method. Now his successors turned Newton's work against him. If aether could be investigated it must be material, and initiate motion in other bodies by mechanical impulse. Hence it became known that in his later writings Newton had endorsed a kind of matter whose activity was internal and self-sustaining. With such a principle, the universe had no need of a God. Sir Isaac Newton's philosophy 'led in its consequences' to atheism.

At the beginning of the eighteenth century the mathematical description of the universe of *Principia* began to be taught throughout Europe. It had a particular place in the curriculum at Coleridge's school, Christ's Hospital, where the mathematics teacher during Coleridge's years was William Wales, FRS, one of the finest astronomers of the age, who had circumnavigated the globe with James Cook between 1772 and 1775. As Master of the King's Naval School at Christ's Hospital, Wales had the responsibility for teaching boys who would one day lead the country's navy. The young Coleridge thus learned of the concise and austere mathematical description of the world of *Principia*, and the precise laws of matter-in-motion, which in his maturity he would reject and which his friend would call 'a universe of death'.[8]

It did not first appear so. Coleridge's 'Greek Ode on Astronomy' submitted for the Browne Prize for Greek at Cambridge in 1793 readily demonstrates the poet's confidence that Newton's mathematical system would uphold and further the truths of natural religion:

> There, Priest of Nature! dost thou shine,
> NEWTON! a King among the Kings divine.
> Whether with harmony's mild force,
> He guides along its course

of the Book entituled *Commercium Epistolicum Collinii et aliorum, De Analysi promota*; published by order of the *Royal-Society*, in relation to the Dispute between Mr. *Leibnitz* and Dr. *Keill*, about the Right of invention of the Method of *Fluxions*, by some call'd the *Differential Method*', *Phil. Trans.* xxix (1714–16) 223–4).

[8] 'The tendency, too potent in itself, / Of habit to enslave the mind—I mean / Oppress it by the laws of vulgar sense, / And substitute a universe of death, / The falsest of all worlds, in place of that / Which is divine and true' (Wordsworth, *The Prelude* (1805) xiii. 138–43, in *The Prelude 1799, 1805, 1850*, ed. J. Wordsworth, M. H. Abrams, and S. Gill (New York and London, 1979), 466).

> The axle of some beauteous star on high,
>   Or gazing, in the spring
>   Ebullient with creative energy,
> Feels his pure breast with rapturous joy possest,
> Inebriate in the holy ecstasy.   (96–104)[9]

This is a standard hymn to genius, and shows no critical insight into Newton's work. Its model could well have been James Thomson's 'Ode on the Death of Sir Isaac Newton' (1727):

>   an harmonious system—all combined,
> And ruled unerring by that single power
> Which draws the stone projected to the ground.
>   O unprofuse magnificence divine!
> O wisdom truly perfect! thus to call
> From a few causes such a scheme of things,
> Effects so various, beautiful, and great,
> An universe complete!   (65–72)

Not until the spring of 1795, several months after leaving Cambridge, did Coleridge begin to study Newton's philosophy critically.

The Bristol public lectures that were to pay for Coleridge's ticket to Pennsylvania were titled 'Lectures on Revealed Religion'. His published notes, however, make it clear that large parts of the lectures concerned natural religion. In the first lecture, Coleridge set his sights on the pantheists. They were 'atheists' who have

substituted certain plastic Natures as inherent in each particle of Matter— certain inconceivable Essences that are, as it were, the unthinking Souls of each atom! But how these Unthinking Essences came to agree among each other so as by their different & opposite operations to form one Whole is a Mystery . . . (*Lectures 1795*, 98–9)

In *The True Intellectual System* Cudworth had attacked what he called 'hylozoic materialism' for denying that the fragmentary activity, internal to matter, was controlled by a higher principle of action. Coleridge summarized these arguments in 'Remarks &c on Atheism':

The second species of atheists are those who like the former affirm that all things are material, but attribute to the *atoms* or matter not only moveability but a self-motive power—and not only substance, figure, and

---

[9] This poem survives only in a translation by Southey of 1802. See Beer, *Coleridge the Visionary*, 74–5 for this poem as a hymn to genius.

situation, but life and appetences—to all atoms life, and to different atoms different appetences & powers of election—making conscious[ness] & reasoning result, not as an accident or mode of these atoms organized, but as the aggregate of their essential qualities—made perceptible, & not given, by this aggregation. (BL MS Egerton 2801, fol. 215)

To support his argument against the pantheists, Coleridge borrowed Colin Maclaurin's enthusiastic summary of Newton's system, *An Account of Sir Isaac Newton's Philosophical Discoveries* (1748). Maclaurin defended the aether theory:

Tho' [God] . . . is the source of all efficacy, yet we find that place is left for second causes to act in subordination to him . . . If, for example, the most noble phaenomena in nature be produced by a rare elastic *aetherial medium*, as Sir *Isaac Newton* conjectured, the whole efficacy of this medium must be resolved into his power and will, who is the supreme cause. . . . It is easy to see that this conjecture no way derogates from the government and influences of the Deity . . . (pp. 388–9)

This evidently satisfied the lecturer. The aether theory postulates activities within nature which are tiny sparks of divine action, yet the being of the deity remains distinct from the aetherial medium, and unchanged by its action. Newton was not a deist. 'Sir Isaac Newton', Coleridge lectured, 'employed his patient Industry and lynx-eyed Penetration in discovering how the World had been constituted and having in part developed it he was soon able to prove that as it was made, so it ought to have been!'[10]

But Coleridge was not long satisfied. Sometime after April 1795 he began to help Southey revise the proofs of his political poem *Joan of Arc*, which retold the events in fifteenth-century France to attack the enemies of eighteenth-century revolutionary France. The English warred against the visionary Maid of Orleans, ran the argument of the poem, because their society was corrupt and they had no perception of the truth. The English were warring against the French Republic in 1795 for the same reason. Coleridge was struck by his friend's thesis and worked hard on the revisions. But he also persuaded Southey to let him write a critique of the nation of 'practical Atheists',[11] as he called the British. Seeking to understand why Britons were fighting to prevent the collapse of Old Corruption, Coleridge looked for the roots of this 'practical atheism' and found

---

[10] *Lectures 1795*, 189.   [11] Ibid. 58.

them in the writings of the most influential English philosopher of
the age. 'It has been asserted', he wrote rather grandly in his long
footnote to *Joan of Arc*, ii. 34, 'that Sir Isaac Newton's philosophy
leads in its consequences to Atheism: perhaps not without reason':

> some there are who deem themselves most free,
> When they within this gross and visible sphere
> Chain down the winged thought, scoffing ascent
> Proud in their meanness: and themselves they cheat
> With noisy emptiness of learned phrase,
> Their subtle fluids, impacts, essences,
> Self-working Tools, uncaus'd Effects, and all
> Those blind Omniscients, those Almighty Slaves,
> Untenanting Creation of its God.
>
> (*Joan of Arc*, ii. 29–37)

Years later Coleridge remembered reading the book which had
caused his revaluation of Newton's philosophy: 'by the bye, I must
get the Book—which I have never seen since in my 24th year I walked
with Southey on a desperate hot Summerday from Bath to Bristol
with a Goose, 2 vol. of Baxter on the Immortality of the Soul, and
the Giblets, in my hand'.[12]

In *An Enquiry into the Nature of the Human Soul*[13] Andrew
Baxter had set out to show that immaterial substance (i.e. spirit) was
the cause of all spontaneous motions in the world. He attacked all
'materialist' philosophies from Lucretius to Spinoza which claimed
to explain order solely in terms of matter, and he also examined
Newton's account of the 'subtile fluid' aether:

*The powers of gravity, elasticity, repulsion, attraction, can no more be lodged
in the matter of this fluid than in the matter of the real bodies we have been
speaking of* . . . for this is as contradictory in respect of one sort of matter
as another, in respect of a very small particle as of a much greater one, being
a palpable contradiction in respect of all matter equally. The matter of this
fluid then being, in all respects, matter that resists a change of its state, we
must still as much seek a cause of its motion *ab extra* to it, that is, in effect,
in *something not matter*, in some immaterial cause, or being . . . (i. 30–1)

---

[12] Notebook 35.36, quoted from J. Beer, *Coleridge's Poetic Intelligence* (London,
1977), 79.

[13] *An Enquiry into the Nature of the Human Soul; wherein the Immateriality of
the Soul Is evinced from the Principles of Reason and Philosophy* [1733]. As the
1st edn. is a single-volume folio, I quote from the 3rd edn., 2 vols. (1745).

Baxter was one of the 'dualist' moderns: things are either material and inert, or immaterial and active. Newton's account of aether plainly shows that it is material; thus it cannot be the cause of motion. Indeed, as an active but material principle it is actually self-contradictory. Coleridge copied a passage into his *Joan of Arc* footnote where Baxter argues that the operations of aether would not produce the observed phenomena of motion, but opposite effects.[14] Yet by making the method of action of aether so thoroughly mechanical, Baxter, and thus Coleridge, miss their target, for Newton would merely have denied that he had conceived aether to act with mechanical force.

Believing that Baxter had exposed aether as 'active matter', Coleridge's conclusion was inevitable:

> It has been asserted that Sir Isaac Newton's philosophy leads in its consequences to Atheism: perhaps not without reason. For if matter by any powers or properties *given* to it, can produce the order of the visible world, and even generate thought; why may it not have possessed such properties by *inherent* right? and where is the necessity of a God? matter is, according to the mechanic philosophy capable of acting most wisely and most beneficently without Wisdom or Benevolence; and what more does the Atheist assert? if matter possess those properties, why might it not have possessed them from all eternity? Sir Isaac Newton's Deity seems to be alternately operose and indolent; to have delegated so much power as to make it inconceiveable what he can have reserved. He is dethroned by Vice-regent second causes. (*Joan of Arc*, ii. 34 n.)

This is a Platonic argument: wise and beneficent action is not possible without the existence in the universe of Wisdom and Beneficence: if it is not accepted, the system Coleridge attributed to Newton is perfectly consistent. But Newton would never have accepted that system, for he had consistently rejected the idea that the order of nature could have arisen without the divine mind acting as designer and protoplast. Coleridge's only real attack on Newton in this passage is the argument that God is so powerful that he could act directly in nature without delegating so much power to intermediates to make him 'operose and indolent'. But it does not follow that God

---

[14] Coleridge has been charged with plagiarism in this footnote: 'the whole note . . . was an unacknowledged condensation from Andrew Baxter' (Fruman, *Coleridge*, 131, 479). This is, however, untrue: Coleridge correctly acknowledges Hartley and Baxter in the first half of the footnote, while the remainder is his own work.

will act directly, merely because he *can*, and there may be reasons unknown to man why a chain of intermediates between God and the world form the best system. Maclaurin had already given one reason for a 'chain of nature' when he wrote that 'the higher we rise in the scale of nature, towards the supreme cause, the views we have . . . appear more beautiful and extensive.'[15] Elsewhere Coleridge seems to agree with this, for when he lectured on the Slave Trade in June he noted how 'fixing our eye on the glittering Summits that rise one above the other in Alpine endlessness . . . [Imagination] still urges us up the ascent of Being, amusing the ruggedness of the road with the beauty and grandeur of the ever-widening Prospect.'[16] He is in fact glorifying the 'littleist' approach he was later to condemn.

In the final paragraph of his footnote, Coleridge gave an impressive and original account of the dilemma which faced the seeker after causes:

We seem placed here to acquire a knowledge of *effects*. Whenever we would pierce into the *Adyta* of Causation, we bewilder ourselves; and all, that laborious Conjecture can do, is to fill up the gaps of imagination. We are restless, because *invisible* things are not the objects of vision — and philosophical systems, for the most part, are received not for their Truth, but in proportion as they attribute to Causes a susceptibility of being *seen*, whenever our visual organs shall have become sufficiently powerful.

Although he attributed 'active matter' and thus atheism to Newton, Coleridge actually shared much with the speculative philosopher of the aether. He was, of course, as restless as Newton to explore the inner sanctum of Causation, and his criticism is of the empiricists' unwillingness to base their accounts of causation on any other than grounds which were observable. Coleridge's final criticism of Newton is acute, for the main problem the philosopher faced in describing the cause of motion in the world was how he could resolve his Neoplatonic belief in 'active' nature with his empirical method. By straying too far towards proofs in his published accounts of aether, the active principle was inevitably perceived as part of the visible, material world, and so condemned.

Now that he had highlighted the mistakes in Newton's system, it seemed appropriate to correct them. This is the second draft of

---

[15] *An Account of Sir Isaac Newton's Philosophical Discoveries*, 389.
[16] *Lectures 1795*, 235.

Coleridge's poem 'Effusion xxv' written in August 1795, which in 1817 became 'The Eolian Harp':[17]

> And what if All of animated Life
> Be but as Instruments diversly fram'd
> That tremble into thought, while thro' them breathes
> One infinite and intellectual Breeze?
> [In diff'rent ⟨Heights so⟩ aptly ⟨hung,⟩ that
> Half-heard Murmurs and loud Bursts sublime,
> Shrill Discords and most soothing Melodies
> ⟨Raise one⟩ great harmonious Concert
> Thus God the only universal Soul,
> ⟨Mechaniz'd Matter⟩ the ⟨Organic⟩ Harps,*
> And each one's Tunes are that, which each calls I. *del.*]
> And all in different Heights so aptly hung,
> ⟨That⟩ Murmurs indistinct and Bursts sublime,
> Shrill Discords and most soothing Melodies,
> Harmonious from Creation's vast concent?
> Thus *God* would be the universal Soul,
> Mechaniz'd matter ⟨as⟩ th'organic harps,
> And each one's Tunes be that, which each calls *I.* —
>
> *Organiz'd Body as Instruments
>
> ('Rugby MS', fols. 31–2)

In the published version of April 1796 the draft was shortened to:

> And what if all of animated nature
> Be but organic Harps diversly fram'd,
> That tremble into thought, as o'er them sweeps
> Plastic and vast, one intellectual Breeze,
> At once the Soul of each, and God of all?   (44–8)

The draft's 'animated Life' was changed to 'animated nature' in the published version, as the poet emphasized that he was speculating on God's relation to the whole of creation, not simply those parts traditionally imbued with the spark of vitality. Matter is passive and 'organic', that is, specifically designed as an instrument to respond to the activity of God, whose action in the world is manifest in the 'infinite and intellectual Breeze'. Like Newton, Coleridge reveals his thoughts more readily in manuscript than in print, for the draft

---

[17] This draft was published (with transcription errors) in *The Complete Poetical Works of Samuel Taylor Coleridge*, ed. E. H. Coleridge, 2 vols. (Oxford, 1912), ii. 1022–3.

presents a hierarchy of principles which does not appear in the final version. God, in the innermost sanctuary, acts in the wholly immaterial realm of Mind, and his activity is transferred downwards to matter through an imponderable active principle, the 'intellectual Breeze', which, like Newton's aether, is the *archē* between the worlds of spirit and matter. Coleridge's draft, moreover, refers to the 'chain of being', for it assigns each to a particular place in the hierarchy: 'in different Heights so aptly hung'. At first this active principle breathes 'thro'' nature and, like the Platonists' 'plastic power' is in the closest union with organic matter as an internal power which acts from within. In the published poem, however, it 'sweeps o'er' the organic harps: the change more clearly emphasizing passive material principles, to avoid the idea of active matter and the poet's own charge against Newton. The same danger is apparent in this passage from Cudworth, which has been seen as a source of the poetry:

> if the musical art were conceived to be immediately in the instruments and strings, animating them as a living soul, and making them to move exactly, according to the laws of harmony, without any external impulse: these, and such like instances . . . would be fit iconisms or representations of *the plastick nature*, that *being art it self acting immediately upon the matter as an inward principle in it.* (*True Intellectual System*, i. 115)[18]

Out of context it is possible to interpret Cudworth's conception of the activity of nature as an activity of inherent right, like aether dependent on nothing other than itself. As Cudworth, Newton, and Coleridge run into similar difficulties in conveying the deity's relation to the world, it is likely that whatever differences they perceived in each other, their conceptions of nature were actually very similar.

In the first chapter of this study I suggested that in *Religious Musings* Coleridge portrays a line of ancient philosophers, including Newton, who had preserved a body of revealed knowledge, including the idea of the 'one supreme Deity'. A close reading of *Religious Musings*, however, reveals that the poet strays from strict Unitarianism to speculate on the intermediate principles of divine action in the world. Early in the poem the elect band view a Platonic Trinity:

> Him, Nature's Essence, Mind, and Energy! (55)

---

[18] C. G. Martin, 'Coleridge and Cudworth: A Source for "The Eolian Harp" ', *Notes and Queries*, ccxi (1966), 173–6, and H. W. Piper, ' "The Eolian Harp" Again', ibid. ccxiii (1968), 23–5, discuss the source.

This is a Platonic Trinity, for the relation of 'Mind' to 'Essence' is wholly self-contemplative: 'Mind' actively reads its own eternal attributes in 'Essence' before translating them into the world through 'Energy', the third member of the divine trinity. 'Energy' is thus the 'intellectual Breeze' of 'The Eolian Harp', Cudworth's *plastick nature*, and it appears to be wholly immaterial, having no resemblance to Newton's aether with its imponderable status between matter and spirit.

Later in *Religious Musings*, the 'Energy' of the deity becomes a plurality of 'plastic powers', and is much closer to the aether hypothesis:

> And ye of plastic power, that interfus'd
> Roll thro' the grosser and material mass
> In organizing surge! Holies of God!   (423–5)

Instead of a unified ubiquitous spirit, there are many principles, which being less 'gross' than the 'material mass', take on the status of imponderable agents, hovering like aether between matter and spirit.

Thus like aether itself, Coleridge's conception of the animating force of the universe wavers between material and immaterial, unity and diversity. When he considers God's action in the world, the causal principle is elevated to the third member of the divine trinity, in a Platonic hierarchy of God's attributes. But seen from nature as the immanent causal power in the world, it is a finely divided active substance, intimately connected with the materials it animates.

Coleridge attempted to reconcile his two perceptions of God's activity in *Joan of Arc*:

> Infinite myriads of self-conscious minds
> Form one all-conscious Spirit . . .
>   . . . yet *seem*
> With various province and apt agency
> Each to pursue its own self-centering end.
>
>   (44–5, 47–9, my emphasis)

Here he suggests that it is a question of perception. In the unchanging world, God acts ubiquitously through his spirit, inspiring and activating matter to all forms of motion. From man's world and his partial vision these activities are perceived as the self-sustaining and independent forces of heat, magnetism, electricity, chemical action, and gravitation:

> Some nurse the infant diamond in the mine;
> Some roll the genial juices thro' the oak;
> Some drive the mutinous clouds to clash in air;
> And rushing on the storm with whirlwind speed
> Yoke the red lightning to their vollying car   (50–4)

Coleridge is struggling with two different ways of looking at nature's activity. Either there is one all-pervading divine principle which causes matter to act in unique ways because each is tuned to a different level; or there are many active principles, each working to a different purpose within nature. In *Joan of Arc* the diversity of these activities in the four realms of earth, water, air, and fire is portrayed, and Coleridge suggests that though they seem to bear no resemblance to one another, they form 'one all-conscious Spirit' by an overall unity of purpose. The same idea re-emerges at the end of *Religious Musings*:

> Contemplant Spirits! ye that hover o'er
> With untir'd gaze th'immeasurable fount
> Ebullient with creative Deity!
>
> . . . . . .
>
> (And what if Monads of the infinite Mind?)   (422–2, 6)

Here the phrase 'And what if' alerts the reader to the moment of highest speculative thought in the poem, recalling a similar moment in 'The Eolian Harp': 'And what if all of animated nature . . .'.

In these three poems written within months of each other Coleridge thus attempted to describe one of the oldest and most difficult of metaphysical problems in the relationship between the supreme unity of the Godhead and the dynamism and diversity of the material world.

After the publication of the *Opticks* in 1704 Newton became interested in the corpuscularian theory of matter, first stated by the Greeks Democritus and Epicurus, and then revived in the seventeenth century by Pierre Gassendi and others. Supporters of this philosophy, known usually as materialists or atomists, believed that the ultimate units of matter were minute spherical particles, all of which had identical shape, size, and mass. Different materials had different densities, but as all atoms were identical the atomists argued that less dense bodies must contain more space in their internal structure and were thus more porous than materials with greater densities.

By 1704 Newton believed that all common forces (gravity, magnetism, electricity, light, and chemical attraction) were transmitted through matter and space by way of the imponderable fluid aether. The idea that matter was porous suited his observations that aether could act through bodies without any diminution or loss of effect (for example, light could travel through some bodies for substantial distances). Newton suggested that even dense bodies might have an atomic arrangement that allowed a considerable amount of empty space. The 1717 edition of the *Opticks* thus dealt with bodies being 'much more rare and porous than is commonly believed':

How Bodies can have a sufficient quantity of Pores for producing these Effects is very difficult to conceive, but perhaps not altogether impossible. . . . if we conceive these Particles of Bodies to be so disposed amongst themselves, that the Intervals or empty Spaces between them may be equal in magnitude to them all; and that these Particles may be composed of other Particles much smaller, which have as much empty Space between them as equals all the Magnitudes of these smaller Particles: And that in like manner these smaller Particles are again composed of others much smaller, all which together are equal to all the Pores or empty Spaces between them; and so on perpetually till you come to solid Particles . . . (pp. 268–9)

Newton was characteristically reticent about making known his ideas on the internal structure of matter. By the 1720s, however, his views on atomism were being spread by pupils like Henry Pemberton, who wrote the first popular treatise of the Newtonian system, *A View of Sir Isaac Newton's Philosophy* (1728). 'This whole globe of earth, nay all the known bodies in the universe together,' Pemberton wrote, 'may be compounded of no greater a portion of solid matter, than might be reduced into a globe of one inch only in diameter, or even less.'[19] In his *Letters Concerning the English Nation* Voltaire also noted this extraordinary consequence of what had become known as Newton's 'doctrine of pores': 'examining the vast Porosity of Bodies, every Particle having its Pores, and every Particle of those Particles having its own; he shows we are not certain that there is a cubic Inch of solid Matter in the Universe, so far are we from conceiving what Matter is.'[20]

Coleridge knew of Newton's 'doctrine of pores', and he understood its implications for matter. In the footnote to *Joan of Arc* he referred to the 'extravagant opinions . . . concerning the progression of pores'.

---

[19] p. 356.   [20] Trans. J. Lockman (London, 1733), 147.

Moreover, entries in his notebook of 1795 show that this aspect of the philosopher's work had caught Coleridge's imagination just as much as the aether hypothesis:

World-[?makers/maker].—
As if according to Sir Isaac Newton's progression of pores—they had coarct the world to a Ball and were playing with it— (*CN* i. 93)

It surely is not impossible that to some infinitely superior being the whole Universe may be one plain—the distance between planet and planet only the pores that exist in any grain of sand—and the distances between system & system no greater than the distance between one grain and the grain adjacent. (*CN* i. 120)

With this belief in the extreme paucity of matter—less than a cubic inch in the entire universe!—and its lowly status at the bottom of the hierarchy of being, it was perhaps inevitable that Newton's universe should be emptied of the small quantity of matter it still contained. A Jesuit priest Roger Boscovich proposed this in his *Theoria Philosophiae Naturalis* (1763), a work later of great importance in the development of the unified field-theory:

The primary elements of matter are in my opinion perfectly indivisible & non-extended points; they are so scattered in an immense vacuum that every two of them are separated from one another by a definite interval; this interval can be indefinitely increased or diminished, but can never vanish altogether without compenetration of the points themselves; for I do not admit as possible any immediate contact between them. (pt. 1, sect. 7; trans. J. M. Child, *A Theory of Natural Philosophy* (Chicago and London, 1922; Cambridge, Mass., 1966), 20)

Boscovich took Newton's idea to its limiting point, making atoms into non-extended centres of force. But he was concerned to preserve matter/spirit dualism in his system, and so stressed the distinction between incorporeal activity in nature and the passivity of the physical point-sources. However, when Joseph Priestley reviewed eighteenth-century debates on matter in *Disquisitions Relating to Matter and Spirit* (1777), he decided that the Jesuit had abolished the distinction between matter and spirit:

The principles of the Newtonian philosophy were no sooner known, than it was seen how few, in comparison of the phenomena of nature, were owing to *solid matter*, and how much to *powers*, which were only supposed to accompany and surround the solid parts of matter. It has been asserted . . . that for any thing we know to the contrary, *all the solid matter in the*

solar system might be contained within a nut-shell [my emphasis], there
is so great a proportion of *void space* within the substance of the most solid
bodies. Now when solidity had apparently so very little to do in the system,
it is really a wonder that it did not occur to philosophers sooner . . . that
there might be no such a thing in nature.

It is maintained, in this treatise . . . that matter is not that *inert* substance
that it has been supposed to be; that *powers of attraction* or *repulsion* are
necessary to its very being . . . And since it has never yet been asserted,
that the powers of *sensation* and *thought* are incompatible with these,
(*solidity*, or *impenetrability* only, having been thought to be repugnant to
them,) I therefore maintain, that we have no reason to suppose that there
are in man two substances so distinct from each other . . . (2nd edn. (1782),
in *Works*, iii. 230, 219)

This conception of matter is most unlike Newton's own. Replacing
'dull' matter on the lowest rung of the ladder of being, Priestley
suggests that powers may be the essence of both matter and mind
and so endorses a materialism in which physical force becomes the
only existing principle in the universe.

Coleridge read Priestley's *Disquisitions* at Cambridge, perhaps
during his last term in the autumn of 1794 when his enthusiasm for,
and proximity to, Dr. Priestley's radical circle was at its height. In
an exuberant letter to Southey in December 1794, Coleridge declared
that he too believed 'in the corporeality of *thought*'.[21] A year later
in *The Plot Discovered*, he made direct reference to the above passage
from *Disquisitions* in a parody of Pitt: 'His style is infinitely porous:
deprived of their vacuities the τὸ πᾶν [the whole], the universe of
his bills and speeches would take up less room than a nutshell.'[22]

Yet as an initial acquaintance with Newton's philosophy had led
to a critical evaluation, so too with Priestley. By the spring of 1795,
when he read the criticism Cudworth had levelled at the ancient and
modern philosophers who claimed intrinsic power as a property
of matter, Coleridge was more guarded about Priestley's active
materialism:

The [Stoics] . . . believed a God indeed or at least seemed to believe one—
but it was a material God, a principle of fire, to which they sometimes

---

[21] *CL* i. 247.

[22] *Lectures 1795*, 296. As far as I am aware this 'nutshell' allusion is the only
direct evidence of Coleridge reading Priestley's influential work. Despite giving
Disquisitions a central role in his discussion of Coleridge's pantheism, Herbert Piper
in *The Active Universe* failed to establish the poet's knowledge of the work.

ascribed Intelligence, and sometimes obscurely denied it—and when they allowed an intelligent God, they by no means supposed him a first Cause, but the result of the organization of the Universe, *in the same manner as our minds have been supposed to be the effect of the peculiar organization of our Bodies.* (*Lectures 1795*, 156; my emphasis)[23]

In place of the Platonic hierarchy Priestley's materialism required only the immediate and immanent agency of God to create, around each mathematical point in space, active powers of attraction and repulsion which gave it the characteristics of matter or spirit. Yet if these points had powers of attracting and repelling, they might possess these by intrinsic right, and so deny the need for a God.[24] Priestley's material points began to look like Newton's aether, for both claim an activity which usurps the deity.

Although Coleridge praises Priestley and criticizes Newton in prose, the reverse is true in his poetry. Each time the organizing principles of the world are discussed, the poet draws a clear distinction between passive matter made of atoms, and spiritual principles which he writes of as composed of monads:[25]

> as one body is the aggregate
> Of atoms numberless, each organiz'd;
> So by a strange and dim similitude,
> Infinite myriads of self-conscious minds
> Form one all-conscious Spirit, who directs
> With absolute ubiquity of thought
> All his component monads . . .
>
> (*Joan of Arc*, ii. 41–7)

> And ye of plastic power, that interfus'd
> Roll thro' the grosser and material mass
> In organizing surge!
>
> (*Religious Musings*, 423–5)

---

[23] Priestley made no serious attempt to demonstrate how his system was compatible with mental powers, relying instead on Locke's argument that 'God can, if he pleases, superadd to matter a faculty of thinking' (*Disquisitions*, in *Works*, iii. 367 n). See Locke, *An Essay Concerning Human Understanding*, bk. IV, ch. 3, sect. 6.

[24] This aspect of Priestley's work has yet to be fully explored: see Heimann and McGuire, 'Newtonian Forces and Lockean Powers'.

[25] '[A] monad is held to be (1) a simple, irreducible, and sometimes indestructible entity; and (2) the minimal unity into which the cosmos and all composite things in it can be resolved; yet (3) containing within itself, in contrast to material atoms, powers and relations of which it is itself the source' (L. E. Loemker, 'Monads and

Early in *Joan of Arc*, Coleridge unambiguously states the fundamental concepts of the Newtonian universe—inert mass and active force:

> But Properties are God: the naked mass
> Acts only by its inactivity.   (38–9)

Matter is impoverished, inactive, and inert until higher principles stimulate it. Over it, or 'interfus'd' through it, are the active units, the monads of God, which direct all motion in the world.

Coleridge took over a system of the world from the seventeenth century that was a complex blend of Neoplatonic hierarchies and Newtonian mechanics, and rejected the more advanced theories of eighteenth-century materialists. His struggles with Newton's philosophy, however, gave his own writing an added subtlety. Seen from the lowly level of the material world, the organizing principles of nature appear self-centred with an internal energy, independent of any higher unity of purpose. But when experienced by a visionary soul from the heights of being, the principle of all activity is perceived as the World-Soul of creation, ubiquitous through every particle of being:

> Glory to thee, FATHER of Earth and Heaven!
> All-conscious PRESENCE of the Universe!
> Nature's vast ever-acting ENERGY!
> In will, in deed, IMPULSE of All to all . . .
>
> (*Joan of Arc*, ii. 442–5)

Monadology', in P. Edwards (ed.), *Encyclopedia of Philosophy*, v (London and New York, 1967), 362).

3

The Elect Band of Patriot Sages

In the Moon is a certain Island near by a mighty continent, which small island seems to have some affinity to England, &, what is more extraordinary, the people are so much alike, & their language so much the same, that you would think you was among your friends.

Blake, 'An Island in the Moon' (satirizing the Lunar Society of
Birmingham)

BY the summer of 1795 Coleridge, the poet and philosopher of human progress, had identified the tradition that had preserved original revealed truths for his own age in the latter days of the world. He had also found in the system of Isaac Newton a metaphysics from which he could develop his own beliefs. But Coleridge did not suppose that he alone was to transform the age. He had to identify other disciples of the truth and to co-ordinate his work with theirs in order to enlighten the modern world. This chapter looks at these young disciples, and how Coleridge made contact with them.

In the Queries which end the 1717 *Opticks* Newton speculated at length about electricity, which he anticipated would prove to be a major principle of action in the universe. At the time small amounts of static electricity could be generated to create amusement in household games, but no one had any conception of the part that these small blue flashes played in the structure of creation. The person to demonstrate this would not only inherit Newton's crown, but would transform natural philosophy. Twenty-five years after the sage's death, a printer from the New World brought about the new age of science:

To demonstrate, in the completest manner possible, the sameness of the electric fluid with the matter of lightning, Dr. Franklin, astonishing as it must have appeared, contrived actually to bring lightning from the heavens, by means of an electrical kite, which he raised when a storm of thunder was perceived to be coming on. This kite had a pointed wire fixed upon it, by which it drew the lightning from the clouds. This lightning descended by the hempen string, and was received by a key tied to the extremity of it; that part of the string which was held in the hand being of silk, that the electric virtue might stop when it came to the key. He found that the string would conduct electricity even when nearly dry, but that when it was wet, it would conduct it quite freely; so that it would stream out plentifully from the key, at the approach of a person's finger. (Priestley, *The History and Present State of Electricity, with Original Experiments* (1767), 179)

These spectacular experiments and his subsequent invention of the lightning conductor made the name of Benjamin Franklin, 'the man who had tamed the might of the heavens', and when he arrived in London in 1757 he was probably the most famous experimental philosopher in the world—the new Newton.[1]

Yet Franklin had not come to Britain as an experimental philosopher, but as chief political emissary of the discontented American States. From 1758 to 1774, when diplomatic measures ceased after the Boston Tea-Party, Franklin led the campaign for reform of the proprietary taxes in America.[2] He also surrounded himself with a group of radical political thinkers who were to have a profound effect on the events in Britain in the latter decades of the eighteenth century.

In 1758 Franklin met two young men experimenting with electricity, Matthew Boulton and Erasmus Darwin, to whom on a later visit he introduced William Small, lately Professor of Natural Philosophy in Virginia. Together they began that most celebrated of provincial scientific societies, the Lunar Society of Birmingham, which came to include Joseph Priestley, Josiah Wedgwood, James Watt, and Thomas Day among its fourteen members.[3] At the Royal Society Franklin also met John Canton and Richard Price, both American sympathizers, and through them he was introduced to Joseph Priestley, then a young teacher in the Dissenting Academy at Warrington. Stimulated by meeting the world's greatest electrician, this young Dissenter began to write a history of the science, for which he was required to repeat many of the alleged discoveries. When *The History and Present State of Electricity* was published in 1767 it contained several important new discoveries by its author, and the success of

---

[1] See I. B. Cohen, *Franklin and Newton: An Inquiry into Speculative Newtonian Experimental Science and Franklin's Work in Electricity as an Example Thereof* (Philadelphia, Pa., 1956), 81–2, 511.

[2] Franklin came to Britain to negotiate with the Pennsylvania proprietors Thomas and Richard Penn, and officials of the British government on the issue of taxing proprietary estates in common with other property.

[3] R. E. Schofield, *The Lunar Society of Birmingham: A Social History of Provincial Science and Industry in Eighteenth-Century England* (Oxford, 1963), 26–38.

his work encouraged Priestley to pursue a career in experimental philosophy which was to lead to his discovery of oxygen, photosynthesis, and thus the 'economy of nature'. When he moved to Birmingham in 1780 and began to attend the meetings held 'at the full moon', Priestley merely cemented a bond that already existed through Benjamin Franklin.

As the rift between the American colonies and the British government grew wider, Franklin looked for support to the radical 'coffee-house' societies that flourished in London in the 1760s and 1770s. By his own admission, Franklin's favourite was the 'Club of Honest Whigs' which included William Watson, FRS, James Boswell, John Canton, FRS, and five leading Dissenters: Joseph Priestley, FRS, Richard Price, FRS, Andrew Kippis, FRS, James Burgh, FRS, and Theophilus Lindsey.[4] From such clubs grew the British campaign to support the colonists, and so the English 'Friends of Liberty'. The roles of attenders at these clubs and societies clearly shows the interrelation of experimental philosophy and dissenting Christianity which was to be so important to Coleridge a generation later.

The conjunction of natural philosopher, Dissenter, and political radical at this time is no coincidence. To dissent from the Articles of the Church of England in the eighteenth century involved automatic exclusion from civil and municipal office under the Test and Corporation Acts, and it also excluded a Dissenter and his sons from university education. In place of the universities the Dissenters had established Teaching Academies, where standards often rivalled the older institutions and where, unlike the universities, the modern disciplines such as mechanics, electrostatics, and chemistry were encouraged. Such an education, without the subsequent distraction of the civil professions, allowed Dissenters to establish a significant presence in commerce and manufacturing, and they played a crucial part in the first phase of the industrialization of the country.[5] The Lunar Society members illustrate this, for while all were eminent scientists and, between them, transformed the manufacturing base

---

[4] V. W. Crane, 'The Club of Honest Whigs: Friends of Science and Liberty', *William and Mary Quarterly*, 3rd ser. xxiii (1966), 210–33. The most complete list of members of the club is given by D. O. Thomas, *The Honest Mind: The Thought and Work of Richard Price* (Oxford, 1977), 142–3.

[5] The Academies were also noted centres of radicalism: see A. Lincoln, *Some Political and Social Ideas of English Dissent 1763–1800* (Cambridge, 1938), 66–100.

of Birmingham and the West Midlands, only three had attended English universities.[6]

As the members of the scientific societies and reforming clubs gained fame as philosophers and notoriety as radicals, they won the collective name of 'rational Dissenters'. A religious dissenter is someone who believes that only Christ, and no temporal power, is the sole head of the Church, and that only the Scriptures can guide faith and practice, which must remain matters of private judgement.[7] Many of those called 'rational Dissenters' in the 1770s and 1780s were religious Dissenters in the above sense, but what united them was political dissent with the British government over the American issue. Only with the end of the War of Independence did the group turn its attention to the repeal of the century-old discriminatory Acts which denied civil liberties to those who dissented from the Articles of the Church of England.

There can be little confusion however, about the optimistic rationalism of the group:

let the inquirer take it for granted previously, that every thing is right . . . that is, let him, with a pious confidence, seek for benevolent purposes, and he will be always directed to the right road; and after a due continuance in it, attain to some new and valuable truth: whereas every other principle and motive of examination, being foreign to the great plan on which the universe is constructed, must lead into endless mazes, errors, and perplexities. (Priestley, *History and Present State of Electricity*, p. xxi)[8]

It is this extraordinary confidence in the plan of nature which led Priestley and men like him to the fundamental discoveries of the late eighteenth century. More striking still, though, was the rational Dissenters' perception of the parallel that could be made between their work as natural philosophers and experimentalists, and their hopes for political and social reform. This is well illustrated by the

[6] Fellows of the Royal Society in the Lunar Society were Joseph Priestley, Erasmus Darwin, Josiah Wedgwood, James Watt, Matthew Boulton, James Keir, William Withering, John Whitehurst, Robert Lovell Edgeworth, Samuel Galton, and Robert Augustus Johnson. The other 3 members were William Small, Thomas Day, and Jonathan Stokes. See R. E. Schofield, 'The Lunar Society and the Industrial Revolution', *Univ. Birm. Hist. J.* xi (1967), 94–119.

[7] David Bogue and James Bennett, *History of Dissenters, from the Revolution in 1688, to the Year 1808*, 4 vols. (1808–12), i. 292–303.

[8] Priestley is quoting Hartley, *Observations on Man, his Frame, his Duty, and his Expectations*, 2 vols. (1749), ii. 246.

work of Richard Price, the rational Dissenter who led the English defence of the American rebels.

In 1776 Price published a pamphlet on the right of the colonists to self-government called *Observations on the Nature of Civil Liberty, the Principles of Government, and the Justice and Policy of the War with America*, which sold an enormous 60,000 copies in two years. Although his argument is founded on libertarian principles, his view of America was Utopian, for Price saw America as the New Society where people would enjoy a level of personal and civil freedom only dreamed of in the Old World. Writing to Franklin in April 1784, after Independence for America had been established, Price declared: 'I look upon the Revolution there as one of the most important events in the History of the World.'[9] In a pamphlet of that year, *Observations on the Importance of the American Revolution, and The Means of making it a Benefit to the World*, Price explicitly linked scientific and social progress. Who can doubt, he suggests, that with leaders such as Franklin who have actually seen into the structure of the universe, a better sort of society is being forged?

With heart-felt satisfaction, I see the revolution in favour of universal liberty which has taken place in *America*;—a revolution which opens a new prospect in human affairs, and begins a new aera in the history of mankind . . . Who could have thought, in the first ages of the world, that mankind would acquire the power of determining the distances and magnitudes of the sun and planets?—Who, even at the beginning of this century, would have thought, that, in a few years, mankind would acquire the power of subjecting to their wills the dreadful force of lightening . . . (rev. edn. (1785), 1–2, 5 n.)

When Coleridge went up to Cambridge in October 1791 Benjamin Franklin was dead, Price was dying, and the confident circle of rational Dissent had been shattered by the Birmingham Riot in July of that year when a mob had destroyed Priestley's house and laboratory in revenge for what were described as 'anti-loyalist' writing and preaching.

By coincidence the obituary of the first generation of Dissenter-philosophers had just been published. 'The Economy of Vegetation', the first volume of Erasmus Darwin's *The Botanic Garden*, is an

---

[9] Quoted in Thomas, *Honest Mind*, 264.

extended poem in rhyming couplets which gives, in copious footnotes, a history of progress in each branch of natural philosophy over the century, and in particular the discoveries of Darwin's own circle of Dissenting philosophers, the Lunar Society. In the poem Darwin gave particular prominence to his old mentor, 'immortal Franklin'[10] who first had 'taught us to defend houses and ships and temples from lightning',[11] and subsequently had defeated the 'Tyrant-Power'[12] of England:

> You led your FRANKLIN to your glazed retreats,
> Your air-built castles, and your silken seats;
> Bade his bold arm invade the lowering sky,
> And seize the tiptoe lightnings, ere they fly;
> O'er the young Sage your mystic mantle spread,
> And wreath'd the crown electric round his head. —
> — The patriot-flame with quick contagion ran,
> Hill lighted hill, and man electrifed man;
> Her heroes slain awhile COLUMBIA mourn'd,
> And crown'd with laurels LIBERTY return'd.
>
> (i. 383–8, ii. 367–70)

When Coleridge considered the elect tradition of philosophers and social reformers in *Religious Musings* he gave Benjamin Franklin the central role. In this poem the rational Dissenters are Franklin's disciples:

> O'er waken'd realms Philosophers and Bards
> Spread in concentric circles . . .
>   . . . they who long
> Enamoured with the charms of order hate
> Th'unseemly disproportion; and whoe'er
> Turn . . .
>   . . . to muse
> On that blest triumph, when the PATRIOT SAGE*
> Call'd the red lightnings from th'o'er rushing cloud
> And dashed the beauteous Terrors on the earth
> Smiling majestic.
>
> *DR FRANKLIN
>
> (*Religious Musings*, 239–50)

---

[10] '*Economy of Vegetation*', ii. 356.   [11] Ibid. i. 383 n.
[12] Ibid. ii. 362

The poem continues by identifying the followers of Franklin's experiments in electricity as the political sages who are to reconstruct society:

> These hush'd awhile with patient eye serene
> Shall watch the mad careering of the storm;
> Then o'er the wild and wavy chaos rush
> And tame the outrageous mass, with plastic might
> Moulding Confusion to such perfect forms,
> As erst were wont, bright visions of the day! (256–61)

Not until he stopped at Derby in January 1796 to pay homage to Darwin, did Coleridge meet one of the survivors of Franklin's original circle of rational Dissenters. Yet in the early months of 1795, when he drafted the first version of *Religious Musings*, Coleridge had met a number of the sons and close acquaintances of the Dissenters, and was also known to those who were then leading the British radical movement. It was such men whom Coleridge was to enlist as an elect band of sages to revive for the modern world the ancient revealed truths.

At Cambridge Coleridge met the Steward of Jesus College William Frend, who was well connected to the old radical tradition and was already in trouble with the college for his dissenting views. He and another Cambridge Dissenter, Robert Garnham of Trinity College, had collaborated with Priestley on a new translation of the Bible which was burnt during the Birmingham riot. He had also acted as a guardian for Priestley's younger son while both were travelling through Europe during the troubled year of 1789.[13]

Frend is first mentioned in Coleridge's letters in his second term at Jesus College. Writing to his brother the Revd George Coleridge on 24 January 1794, Coleridge declared: 'Mr Frend's company is by no means invidious. On the contrary, Pierce himself [the Master of Jesus College] is very intimate with him. No! Tho' I am not an *Alderman*, I have yet *prudence* enough to *respect* that *gluttony of Faith* waggishly yclept Orthodoxy.'[14] This was not tactful, for brother George was an orthodox minister of the Church of England. 'I am not an *Alderman*', says Coleridge, hinting that he could not have stood for that office because he was now a Dissenter. This

---

[13] F. Knight, *University Rebel: The Life of William Frend (1757–1841)* (London, 1971), 74–103.
[14] *CL* i. 20

apparent interest in the movement for the repeal of the repressive Test Acts suggests that Coleridge was by then a disciple of Frend, who had campaigned for repeal since finishing his work for Priestley. He was also agitating in Cambridge for the abolition of the slave trade, another major theme of Dissenting protest, and it is significant that Coleridge's prize-winning Greek Ode of 1792 was 'On the Slave-Trade'.

By the end of 1792, Coleridge's fourth term at the university, the news from Paris of massacres had polarized in the town. The octogenarian Henry Gunning remembered that time in his 1854 memoirs:

> Almost every evening during the latter part of this winter [1792–3], there were riotous assemblages, and the windows of many of the Dissenters were broken. A very numerous mob collected one evening, who, after breaking several windows, did great injury to the Meeting-house. . . . An attempt was made in the University and town to represent those who differed from Mr. Pitt as enemies to the constitution. Associations were formed against Republicans and Levellers . . . The Dissenters (as a body) were included in that number . . . (*Reminiscences of the University, Town, and County of Cambridge, from the Year 1780*, 2 vols. (1854), i. 276–8)

Faced with this atmosphere of increasing hostility, in January 1793 Frend wrote *Peace and Union recommended to the Associated Bodies of Republicans and Anti-Republicans*. For most of this pamphlet Frend was conciliatory in tone, but for writing it he was subpoenaed and then expelled from the university. As Frend was finishing the pamphlet, Louis XVI was beheaded in Paris and war with England was declared. His hastily-written appendix had infuriated the university hierarchy:

> Louis Capet was once king of France, and entitled to the honours due to that exalted station. The supreme power in the nation declared, that France should be a republick: from that moment Louis Capet lost his titles. He was accused of enormous crimes, confined as a state prisoner, tried by the national convention, found guilty, condemned, and executed. What is there wonderful in all this? . . . It is in short no business of ours, and if all the crowned heads on the continent are taken off, it is no business of ours . . . (pp. 45–6)

Coleridge's presence at the trial of Frend, who was indicted on a university decree of 1603 against impugning religion, is often mentioned and it should be seen as a strong commitment to the reforming movement even at the risk of his own expulsion from Cambridge. Yet after Frend left Cambridge in August 1793, university life must have become much duller and less relevant for his disciple.

After a seventh term at Jesus College, worried by debts Coleridge decamped from Cambridge to enlist in the Light Dragoons. This folly is well known, but what is not mentioned is the futility Coleridge must have felt at staying in an institution which had expelled his mentor and where his party, the Dissenters, were facing increased hostility. 'In the subsequent winter [1793–4]', Gunning wrote, 'the proceedings of these mobs, (whose watchword was 'Church and King!') were so outrageous, that several Dissenters . . . consulted their own safety by leaving Cambridge for America.'[15] The antipathy Coleridge must have felt towards the university would have been compounded by the fact that he could not have taken his degree without publicly renouncing his Dissenting principles and subscribing to the Articles of the Church of England.

Cambridge survived as a centre of Dissent after Frend's expulsion because of the foundation in June 1793 of the *Cambridge Intelligencer* under the editorship of Benjamin Flower, and by the time Coleridge returned from his sojourn in the army, the Dissenters had reorganized and were disseminating their ideas through the new paper, read nationally, with contributions from Mary Wollstonecraft, William Frend, Mrs Barbauld, Gilbert Wakefield, and eventually Coleridge.[16] This network of Dissenters may have been significant for the ex-soldier. Suddenly there is a new confidence in his correspondence and his circle of acquaintances begins to widen to the Dissenting centres in the Midlands and North.[17]

By the summer of 1794, a year after leaving the university, Frend had become a leading reformer and one of the few of the middle-class rational Dissenters to join forces with the rising generation of radicals led by John Thelwall in the London Corresponding

---

[15] *Reminiscences of Cambridge*, i. 279.

[16] M. J. Murphy, *Cambridge Newspapers and Opinion, 1780–1850* (Cambridge, 1977), 25–42. The first issue of the paper on 20 July 1793 published the Declaration of Rights of the French Convention.

[17] I cannot, however, support the assertion by Robert Owen in his autobiography (*The Life of Robert Owen: Written by Himself* (1857), 36, 70) that Coleridge joined a select club at Manchester in 1793 and there discussed chemistry with John Dalton. See J. Unsworth, 'Coleridge and the Manchester Academy', *Charles Lamb Bulletin*, NS xxx (1980), 149–53.

Society.[18] Coleridge undoubtedly remained in contact with his old mentor: 'To Mr Frend present my most grateful respect—God almighty bless him!'—he wrote to George Dyer in February 1795. It is quite possible that through Frend Coleridge met the radicals' campaign leaders, such as John Thelwall and Joseph Gerrald, when he began his political lecturing in February 1795.

A most important new acquaintance of Coleridge in 1794 was recorded by Henry Gunning:

The topic upon which Coleridge much delighted to converse, was the establishment of a society consisting of twelve members, each of whom . . . should select a highly accomplished woman, who should accompany them to some remote and uninhabited country, where they should form a colony of themselves. . . . The projected colonization never took place, but a button-manufacturer at Birmingham (who was to have been one of the party) defrayed all the expenses that had been incurred to carry out this wild scheme. (*Reminiscences of Cambridge*, i. 300–1)

This is the celebrated scheme of pantisocracy, the Utopian Christian community of which Coleridge and Southey dreamed in correspondence between Cambridge and Oxford in the autumn of 1794. The 'button-manufacturer', as Gunning sneeringly calls him, was none other than the highly-talented, radical, and charismatic James Watt, junior, elder son of Watt the engineer and Lunar Society member. Two years earlier the younger Watt and Thomas Cooper, Priestley's son-in-law, had gained notoriety in Britain by addressing the Club of Jacobins on behalf of the Manchester Constitutional Society. In an impassioned denunciation in the House of Commons, Edmund Burke had accused them of being agents in a conspiracy to promote a federation with the French regicides.[19] Burke's unfounded attack caused Cooper's Manchester business to collapse and brought a charge of treason against Watt's employer Thomas Walker.[20] Faced with the real possibility that a charge of treason would be brought against him if he returned to England, Watt remained in Europe on business for his beleaguered employer and only returned after Walker's acquittal in April 1794. Then, to be safe, his father sent

[18] A. Goodwin, *The Friends of Liberty: The English Democratic Movement in the Age of the French Revolution* (London, 1979), 394.

[19] Ibid. 201–3.

[20] F. Knight, *The Strange Case of Thomas Walker: Ten Years in the Life of a Manchester Radical* (London, 1957), 153–65.

him first to Bristol to Thomas Beddoes, friend of the Lunar Society, and then sought out the patronage of his other business partner and fellow 'Lunatick' Matthew Boulton, a friend of the Prime Minister whose button factory in Birmingham was the largest in Britain.[21]

Thomas Beddoes, who became Coleridge's mentor and doctor, had been Reader in Chemistry at Oxford until his radical sympathies had become unacceptable to that university. Moving to Bristol in 1791, he continued to research in chemistry of gases, developing Priestley's work on the medical properties of airs. By 1794 Beddoes had persuaded James Watt, senior, to design the 'air production' apparatus and was collecting subscriptions for the experimental treatment with gases for a number of incurable illnesses, such as consumption and cancer.[22] When the younger Watt joined him to help with the subscriptions and to keep his bag packed for America in case of a round-up of Dissenters, a centre of radicalism at Bristol seems to have formed around Beddoes, with five young 'rebels'—Watt, Thomas Wedgwood, Robert Lovell, Southey, and Coleridge—regularly in contact.

Henry Gunning remembered that the younger Watt was to have financed the pantisocratic colony on the Susquehanna River and would have joined Coleridge and Southey as one of the twelve. He should probably have credited Watt with much more of the scheme. After the House of Commons 'denouement' Thomas Cooper had decided to leave England and settle in America. In the summer of 1793 he sailed to Pennsylvania with his wife and two brothers-in-law, the sons of Joseph Priestley. Like Coleridge and Southey, Cooper intended to form a colony in Pennsylvania, though not one based on equal ownership. He planned to buy up 300,000 acres of fertile land along the Susquehanna River which he anticipated selling in small lots to his friends the ousted Girondists in Paris and the oppressed radicals in England.[23]

---

[21] P. M. Zall, 'The Cool World of Samuel Taylor Coleridge: Up Loyal Sock Creek', *Wordsworth Circle*, iii (1972), 161–7.

[22] T. H. Levere, 'Dr Thomas Beddoes and the Establishment of his Pneumatic Institution: A Tale of Three Presidents', *Notes and Records of the Royal Society of London*, xxxii (1977), 41–9.

[23] J. R. MacGillivray, 'The Pantisocracy Scheme and its Immediate Background', in M. W. Wallace (ed.), *Studies in English by Members of University College Toronto*, (Toronto, 1931), 153.

In the autumn of 1793 Cooper inspected the land in Pennsylvania and by February 1794 he had enough information to return to England and promote his ideas in *Some Information respecting America*, and in a *Plan de Vente* in Paris.[24] By this time Dr Priestley, tired and abused in London, had also become committed to the scheme. 'At the time of my leaving England', he wrote in his 1795 *Memoirs*, 'my son in conjunction with Mr. Cooper, and other English emigrants, had a scheme for a large settlement for the friends of liberty in general near the head of the Susquehanna in Pennsylvania.'[25] Joseph Priestley, junior, elaborated after his father's death:

I, and some other English gentlemen, had projected a settlement of 300,000 acres of land, about fifty miles distant from Northumberland. The subscription was filled chiefly by persons in England. . . . The scheme of settlement was not confined to any particular class or character of men, religious or political. (*Memoirs of Dr. Priestley*, i. 126)

But the Parisian traveller de Rochefoucauld-Liancourt, who visited Dr Priestley during a trip to America in 1795–6, put a rather different slant on the projected colony:

Having arrived in America some time earlier, his son had bought land, where, under the banner of the Doctor, all the unitarians and other persecuted people from England were to have been reunited. This establishment would have received the protection and honour of the American government, and would have made the Doctor the founder of a colony and the leader of their sect. (*Voyage dans les États-Unis D'Amérique, fait en 1795, 1796 et 1797*, 8 vols. (l'an vii [1799]), i. 129–30; my trans.)

One of the chief recruiters for the colony would have been the younger Watt. He had grown up with Priestley's sons in Birmingham, and his presence in Paris in the early months of 1794 may well have been instrumental for Cooper in launching the ambitious *Plan de Vente*, which envisaged 30 agencies throughout Europe to recruit

[24] *Plan de Vente de Trois Cent Mille Acres de Terres Situées dans les Comtés de Northumberland et de Huntingdon dans l'État de Pensylvanie* (1794). Beneath the title on the copy in the Bibliothèque nationale is written 'Par Mr. Cooper pour Sa Compagnie avec le Dr. Priestley'. See M. W. Kelley, 'Thomas Cooper and Pantisocracy', *Modern Language Notes*, xlv (1930), 218–20.

[25] *Memoirs of Dr. Joseph Priestley, to the year 1795, written by himself: with a continuation, to the time of his decease, by his son, Joseph Priestley* [etc.] 2 vols. (1806–7), i. 126.

the disaffected. Once back in England, as the friend and spokesman of the Susquehanna planners Cooper and Priestley he could have recruited from among the oppressed radicals of his own generation.

The pantisocratic scheme of Southey and Coleridge and the colony of Cooper and Priestley have marked differences, but their coincidence is certainly not accidental. Although Southey had dreamed the year before of a new society, a 'Southeyopolis' where 'ground uncultivated since the creation' existed,[26] it was only when the Bristol circle formed around Beddoes in the early summer of 1794 that pantisocracy became foremost in the minds of Southey, Lovell, and Coleridge.

The three future brothers-in-law were in Bristol writing *The Fall of Robespierre* in August 1794, when another young man of genius visited Beddoes' Pneumatic Institution. He was Thomas Wedgwood, younger son of Josiah Wedgwood, the great chemist, potter, philanthropist, and 'Lunatick'.[27] Wedgwood, who later became Coleridge's patron, had lodged with Watt in Paris during the bloody year of 1792 and he left a clear picture of the character of Watt in a letter to his father: 'I lodge here in the same house with young Watt—he is a furious democrat—detests the King and Fayette. . . . Watt says that a new revolution must inevitably take place, and that it will in all probability be fatal to the King, Fayette, and some hundred others.'[28]

By the time Coleridge returned to Cambridge for his final term at the beginning of September 1794, he had formed a clear idea of how the projected American colony was to work and wrote to Southey: 'Breakfast with Dyer, Author of the Complaints of the Poor . . . I . . . explained our system—he was enraptured—pronounced it impregnable—He is intimate with Dr Priestley—and doubts not, that the Doctor will join us.'[29] But a month later he was tempering

[26] Letters to Grosvenor Bedford, 26 Oct. and 14 Dec. 1793, in Charles Southey (ed.), *The Life and Correspondence of Robert Southey*, 6 vols. (1849–50), i. 187, 196.

[27] Erasmus Darwin wrote to Thomas Wedgwood at 'Tallaton, Ottery St Mary, Devonshire' on 10 Aug. Wedgwood was not, however, staying with Coleridge as King-Hele asserts (*Letters of Erasmus Darwin*, 255–6). Two days later Wedgwood wrote a joint letter with Beddoes to his brother Josiah Wedgwood, which is reproduced in R. B. Litchfield, *Tom Wedgwood: The First Photographer* (London, 1903), 35.

[28] Letter to Josiah Wedgwood, sen., 7 July 1792, quoted in Litchfield, *Tom Wedgwood*, 25–6.

[29] *CL* i. 97–8.

egalitarian idealism with Cooper's commercial realism: 'By all means read & ponder on Cowper — and when I hear your thoughts, I will give you the Result of my own',[30] he told his friend.

It is not possible to know how much mediation there was between the two schemes, and whether 'the Doctor', as Coleridge familiarly called Priestley, and his circle knew anything of the rival scheme of pantisocracy. The symbolic number 'twelve' for the pantisocrats, and their denial of landownership, implies that they were to model their colony on the early Christian communities of the first centuries, though whether their leader was, like Priestley, to be a 'chief of the sect' or a spiritual presence, is not clear.

Cooper and Priestley waited in vain for the French and English radicals to follow them to Pennsylvania.[31] The Girondists went not to America but to the guillotine; while in England, the collapse of the treason trials of the radicals in December 1794 made the country much safer for men like James Watt, who returned to Birmingham and collected subscriptions for Beddoes from among his father's business friends.[32]

Yet the experiences of those months transformed Coleridge. He had met the leaders of the radical movement in England. Alongside them he had planned a new society in the free world, to be peopled with the sages, young and old, who had followed the example of Benjamin Franklin, the first governor of the State they were to settle in. Coleridge left Cambridge without a degree in order to raise money for his new society, but as 1795 progressed, and his lectures became more and more involved in the radical campaign in Britain, his ideas for social and political reform were redirected towards the British radicals and their traditional heartlands in the Midlands and the North.

Religious Musings was written for these young radicals who Coleridge believed were to be the country's future leaders. In the poem they appear as an elect band, the philosophers and sages who have followed the work of Benjamin Franklin, and are now to be instruments in the revolution and transformation of Britain. It is they

[30] 21 Oct.; *CL* i. 115.
[31] Zall ('Cool World', 165–6) suggests that the land in the Susquehanna was found to be quite uninhabitable when the snows melted in the spring of 1795.
[32] See E. Robinson, 'The Origins and Life-Span of the Lunar Society', *Univ. Birm. Hist. J.* xi (1967), 14–15.

                                        who long
Enamoured with the charms of order hate
Th'unseemly disproportion; and whoe'er
Turn with mild sorrow from the victor's car
And the low puppetry of thrones, to muse
On that blest triumph, when the PATRIOT SAGE*
Call'd the red lightnings from th'o'er-rushing cloud
And dashed the beauteous Terrors on the earth
Smiling majestic. Such a phalanx ne'er
Measured firm paces to the calming sound
Of Spartan flute! These on the fated day,
When stung to rage by Pity eloquent men
Have rous'd with pealing voice th'unnumbered tribes
That toil and groan and bleed, hungry and blind—
These hush'd awhile with patient eye serene
Shall watch the mad careering of the storm;
Then o'er the wild and wavy chaos rush
And tame the outrageous mass, with plastic might
Moulding Confusion to such perfect forms,
As erst were wont, bright visions of the day!

                    *DR FRANKLIN

                 (*Religious Musings*, 242–61)

After *Religious Musings* was published in April 1796 Richard Poole
complained to Coleridge that it was too difficult for 'common
readers'. Coleridge was unperturbed: 'the Poem was not written for
common Readers', he wrote.[33] There is every indication that he was
sincere. In the month of publication Coleridge told his publisher
Cottle 'To all the places in the North we will send my Poems',[34] and
he jotted on the manuscript of his collection '250 Birmingham—150
Manchester—80 Liverpool'.[35] He was targeting the poems at those
among whom he had canvassed for *The Watchman* three months
earlier. Here, in the traditional centres of radical dissent, Coleridge
would write his esoteric message for these most uncommon readers.
He had found the band of the elect.

---

[33] *CL* i. 207.   [34] Ibid. 201.   [35] 'Rugby MS', fol. 25

4

How Natural Philosophers Defeated the Whore of Babylon

> I beheld 'a painted patched-up old Harlot.' She was arrayed in purple and scarlet colour, and decked with gold and precious stones and pearls, and upon her Forehead was written 'MYSTERY.'
>
> Coleridge, 'A Letter from Liberty'

IN the early months of 1796 Coleridge made some jottings in his first notebook:

—transfer the proofs of natural to moral Sciences.— (*CN* i. 100)

    Millenium, an History of, as brought about by progression in natural philosophy—particularly, meteorology or science of airs & winds—

    Quare—might not a Commentary on the Revelations be written from late philosophical discoveries? (ibid. 133)

The young poet's interest in the ancient doctrine of the millennium, the seventh and last thousand-year span of the world was certainly not unusual for the end of the eighteenth century.[1] Bishop Ussher's chronology indicated that in 1796 the 6,000-year span of the world had just two hundred years to run (the world will end in 1996). During this latter period calamities had been prophesied to purge the earth for the golden age of the millennium, when, it was believed, Christ would descend in the Second Coming. Many in England had seen in the French Revolutions of 1789 and 1792 the dawn of the latter age, and its bloody progress from the destruction of the Bastille to the Terror was traced by interpreting biblical apocalyptic writing, particularly the Revelation of St John the Divine, where the millennium is described with all attendant commotions. 'I take it that the ten horns of the great beast in revelations, mean the ten crowned heads of Europe', Joseph Priestley wrote to John Adams in America, 'and that the execution of the king of France is the falling off of the first of

---

[1] See W. H. Oliver, *Prophets and Millennialists: The Uses of Biblical Prophecy in England from the 1790s to the 1840s* (Auckland and Oxford, 1978), 11–46.

those horns.'[2] Yet by 1796 it was not possible for many Christians to accept that the atheistic and brutal French Republic was the sole agent of divine providence, and attention had turned from the social order to the natural world, where without doubt God's will prevailed, and his providential design for the universe would unfold.

Other entries in the notebook for 1796 suggest that Coleridge's millenarian thought was influenced by the second volume of Thomas Burnet's *Telluris Theoria Sacra* (1689),[3] written during the time of the last social and political upheaval in the Glorious Revolution of 1688:

> Two of the greatest Speculations that we are capable of in this Life, are, in my Opinion, the REVOLUTION OF WORLDS, and the REVOLUTION OF SOULS; one for the Material World, and the other for the Intellectual. . . . As to the *Revolution* of *Souls*, the footsteps of that Speculation are more obscure than of the former. (Thomas Burnet, *The Theory of the Earth* (etc.), 2 vols. (1684, 1690), vol. ii, part 4, pref.)

Coleridge was evidently reading the original Latin text, for he noted that he intended to translate 'Burnet's Mountains . . . into blank Verse, the original at the bottom of the page'.[4]

The purpose of *Telluris Theoria Sacra* had been to attack the Church of Rome, which Burnet saw as the Whore of Revelations, then ascendant in the reign of James II.[5] Interpreting the biblical Apocalypse as a prophecy of revolution in the natural order, Burnet tried to show that the end of the world was linked to the defeat of Roman Catholicism. Guided by providence, nature was to follow a preordained course that would culminate in a general conflagration, to begin in central Italy (the Vatican, one supposes), the land of volcanoes. At this time Christ would descend from heaven to purge the irreligious States of Europe, the ten-horned Beast of the Apocalypse. Burnet never succeeded in making clear the exact interrelation of political and natural events. In the second volume

---

[2] L.-J. Cappon (ed.), *The Adams-Jefferson Letters: The Complete Correspondence between Thomas Jefferson and Abigail and John Adams*, 2 vols. (Chapel Hill, NC, 1959), ii. 595.

[3] *Telluris theoria sacra: orbis nostri originem et mutationes generales, quas aut iam subiit, aut olim subiturus est, complectens*, 2 vols. (1681, 1689).

[4] I am grateful to John Beer for pointing out the correct reading of this notebook entry, which is misread in CN i. 61. See also CN i. 174 (7), i. 191 n.

[5] See M. C. Jacob and W. A. Lockwood, 'Political Millenarianism and Burnet's *Sacred Theory*', *Science Studies*, ii (1972), 265–79.

of the English revision, published in 1690 after the accession of
William and Mary had removed the Catholic threat James II had
posed, the text became a straightforward description 'of those
extraordinary Phaenomena and Wonders in Nature, that, according
to Scripture, will precede the coming of Christ, and the Conflagration
of the World'.[6] These phenomena were to occur chiefly in the
sphere of Air, which separates Heaven and Earth, and the study of
such aerial phenomena was known to the seventeenth and eighteenth
centuries as 'meteorology or science of airs & winds':[7]

> Let us therefore consider what signs Scripture hath taken notice of, as
> destin'd to appear at that time, to publish, as it were, and proclaim the
> approaching end of the World; And how far they will admit of a natural
> explication, according to those grounds we have already given, in explaining
> the causes and manner of the Conflagration. These Signs are chiefly,
> Earthquakes, and extraordinary commotions of the Seas. Then the darkness
> or bloudy colour of the Sun and Moon; The Shaking of the Powers of
> Heaven, the fulgurations of the Air and the falling of Stars. (*Theory of the
> Earth*, ii. 92–3.)

None of these events had begun in Britain by the end of the eighteenth
century, but several of the poems which Coleridge wrote in the years
1795–6 draw on the spectacular accounts of apocalyptic trials in
The Theory of the Earth, indicating that he, too, anticipated a
spectacular end to the world. An early draft of *Religious Musings*,
which became lines in *Ode to the Departing Year*, follows Burnet's
account of how the Conflagration will occur by the eruption of the
earth's central fires through dried-up seas, to cause fierce and
destructive explosions:

> black *Ruin* sits
> Nursing th'impatient earthquake, and with dreams
> Of shatter'd cities & the promis'd day
> Of central fires thro' nether seas upthundring
> Soothes her fierce solitude —
> (BL Add. MS 35,343, fol. 65; 'Rugby MS', fol. 55)

Yet elsewhere the poet appears to reject this literal rendering of the
Apocalypse, and confines the millenarian revolution to the moral
world, interpreting Revelation figuratively for his own Age:

---

[6] *Theory of the Earth*, ii. 91.   [7] CN 133*b*.

And lo! the Great, the Rich, the Mighty Men,
The Kings and the Chief Captains of the World,
With all that fixed on high like stars of Heaven
Shot baleful influence, shall be cast to earth,
Vile and down-trodden, as the untimely fruit
Shook from the fig-tree by a sudden storm.
Ev'n now the storm begins . . .

(*Religious Musings*, 322–8)

Coleridge footnoted this passage with a quotation from chapter 6 of Revelation and a later reference to the revolution in France makes clear that he was reading the prophecy of St John as an allegory of the 'Revolution of Souls'. Hence he seems inconsistently both to endorse an apocalypse in nature, leading to the destruction of the world and the death of mankind, and a moral revolution, leading to the golden age and a perfect society.[8]

Although Coleridge made use of the imagery in *The Theory of the Earth*, it is clear that he read Burnet for a deeper reason. Like its author, he wished to examine the extent to which the natural world controlled by God could reform or transform the moral world of man. In 1688, deeply dissatisfied with the political and religious life of his age, Burnet had rejected any further improvement in man's earthly condition, and had looked to the end of the old world within 200 years. Coleridge however, makes the extraordinary claim in his note on the millennium that it was the progress in man's knowledge of the science of airs and winds that would bring about the golden age. Hence he differed profoundly from Burnet, for in emphasizing man's progressive understanding of the natural order rather than the evolutionary or apocalyptic course of nature towards a predetermined end, Coleridge implies that as mankind increases in its understanding of the forces and principles that govern nature, human societies will achieve an earthly millennium.

The chief philosopher of human perfectibility in the latter half of the eighteenth century was Joseph Priestley. After publishing *The History and Present State of Electricity* in 1767, he determined to

---

[8] The labels 'pre-' and 'post-millennialist' are used to distinguish between those who believe the second coming will precede the golden age, and those who stress continuity and progressiveness towards the millennium, with the natural apocalypse at some far-distant time; see Oliver, *Prophets and Millennialists*, 20–2. Piper discussed Coleridge's apparent confusion in *Active Universe*, 49–55.

write the entire history of experimental philosophy, believing that 'once the entire progress, and present state of every science shall be fully and fairly exhibited, I doubt not but we shall see a new and capital *aera* commence in the history of all the sciences.'[9] Priestley continued this theme the following year in *An Essay on the First Principles of Government*:

In this state of things, it requires but a few years to comprehend the whole preceding progress of any one art or science . . . If, by this means, one art or science should grow too large for an easy comprehension, in a moderate space of time, a commodious subdivision will be made. Thus all knowledge will be subdivided and extended; and *knowledge*, as Lord Bacon observes, being *power*, the human powers will, in fact, be enlarged; nature, including both its materials and its laws, will be more at our command; men will make their situation in this world abundantly more easy and comfortable; they will probably prolong their existence in it, and will grow daily more happy, each in himself, and more able (and, I believe, more disposed) to communicate happiness to others. Thus whatever was the beginning of this world, the end will be glorious and *paradisiacal*, beyond what our imaginations can now conceive. (*Works*, xxii. 9)

Such a celebration of man's power to control and order nature is to be expected from men who, like Priestley, were at the forefront of the early industrialization of the country. This optimism, originating with Francis Bacon, and so characteristic of the rational Dissenters, became Coleridge's rallying-cry in the Prospectus to *The Watchman*: 'A PEOPLE ARE FREE IN PROPORTION AS THEY FORM THEIR OWN OPINIONS. In the strictest sense of the word KNOWLEDGE IS POWER.' Bacon had believed that through knowledge mankind would gain control of its destiny. 'Freedom through Truth', however, is also the millennial promise of Christ to his disciples in the Gospel of St John. Coleridge took the slogan in its latter sense in *Religious Musings*:

From Avarice thus, from Luxury and War
Sprang heavenly Science: and from Science Freedom.   (237–8)

Led by the disciples of Newton and Franklin, a transformation had occurred in man's knowledge of the 'science of airs & winds' in the eighteenth century, and many became confident that a state of perfect knowledge of the natural world would be achieved within a few decades. The discovery of the identity of electricity and

[9] *History of Electricity*, p. xv.

lightning was of paramount importance, for suddenly many diverse electrical phenomena became intelligible as effects of the motion of the all-pervading aethereal electric fluid. At the time of Franklin's work, church bells were inscribed with legends to defend against electric storms, and were rung at the approach of thunder despite a significant mortality among ringers.[10] But with the invention of the pointed lightning conductor, which both drew and threw off the 'electric fire', one of the world's great natural evils was tamed. Natural events as separate as earthquakes, the growth of plants, sea luminescence, and the shock of the electric eel and fish, were explained on the model of the simple electric capacitor, which stored and discharged static electricity. Some likened the entire world to a capacitor and believed that discharges of electricity were the driving force behind all natural changes in animate and inanimate nature.[11]

Others, like John Wesley, speculated on the medicinal properties of the electric fluid, and hailed electricity as 'the noblest Medicine yet known in the World' and a 'sovereign Remedy', which he deemed to be 'the grand *Desideratum* in Physick, from which we may expect Relief when all other Relief fails'.[12] At St Thomas's Hospital an electrical department was set up, treating paralysis, hysteria, infections, and swellings. By 1793 the London Electrical Dispensary was established. Erasmus Darwin noted in 'The Economy of Vegetation' that electricity could be used to stimulate movement in paralytic limbs. Some treatments, however, were less gentle than others:

Abraham van Doorn . . . threw the boy daily into a tub of water in which a large eel of the black variety was swimming, by which the boy was very strongly shocked and crept out on his hands and feet, but sometimes if he wasn't capable of that he had to be helped . . . The result was a complete cure of the nervous disease, although his thighs remain somewhat swollen as before. (F. van der Lott, 'Kort bericht van den Conger-aal', trans. in Ritterbush, *Overtures to Biology*, 38)

Priestley abandoned the plan for a general review of scientific knowledge in the early 1770s and began the research into the

[10] Cohen, *Franklin and Newton*, 490.
[11] See P. C. Ritterbush, *Overtures to Biology: The Speculations of Eighteenth-Century Naturalists* (New Haven, Conn. and London, 1964), 57–108.
[12] John Wesley, *The Desideratum: or, Electricity Made Plain and Useful* (1760), 72, 70, 43.

chemistry of gases for which he is best remembered. As his six volumes of pneumatic chemistry appeared in the 1770s and 1780s, greatly increasing knowledge of airs, he speculated on uses of the newly discovered substances. 'Fixed air' (carbon dioxide) he first thought was a preventive of scurvy, and he persuaded the Royal Navy to fit carbon-dioxide-producing machines to several ships of the Fleet.[13] The discovery of oxygen gave a significant boost to the idea of pneumatic therapy, and Priestley suggested that oxygen might be used in diseases where atmospheric air was insufficient 'to carry off the phlogistic putrid effluvium fast enough'.[14] But he decided that the use of oxygen should be restricted to medicine, as a healthy person might 'live out too fast' if overexposed to this pure kind of air; although acknowledging that the sense of elevation induced by breathing it made it a potentially 'fashionable article in luxury'.[15]

In the last decade of the eighteenth century Thomas Beddoes became the leading proponent of the new medicine, and in *Considerations on the Medicinal Use of Factitious Airs* (1795), which he published with James Watt, senior, he surveyed the properties of a dozen 'airs', as a prelude to founding his Pneumatic Institution for treatment and investigations. At the end of *A Letter to Erasmus Darwin* (1793) Beddoes expressed his hopes for the new science:

Many circumstances, indeed, seem to indicate that a great revolution in this art is at hand. We owe to PNEUMATIC CHEMISTRY the command of the elements which compose animal substances. Now it is difficult not to believe that much depends on the due proportion of these ingredients; and it is the business of PNEUMATIC MEDICINE to apply them with caution and intelligence to the restoration and preservation of health. — And if you do not, as I am almost sure you do not, think it absurd to suppose the organization of man equally susceptible of improvement from culture with that of various animals and vegetables, you will agree with me in entertaining hopes not only of a beneficial change in the practice of medicine, but in the constitution of human nature itself . . . (59–60)

The medicinal use of airs was too new to be included in Darwin's celebration of scientific progress 'The Economy of Vegetation', but

---

[13] J. G. McEvoy, 'Joseph Priestley, "Aerial Philosopher": Metaphysics and Methodology in Priestley's Chemical Thought, from 1772 to 1781', *Ambix*, xxv (1978), 93–116.
[14] Priestley, *Experiments and Observations on Different Kinds of Air*, 3 vols. (1774–7), ii. 101.
[15] Ibid. 102.

he suggested that advances in the science of 'airs & winds' might bring about paradisiacal conditions by improving the global climate. Noting that polar ice had been shown to be the principal source of coldness in Europe, he first thought that nations might employ their sea-power to navigate these 'immense masses of ice into the more southern oceans'.[16] If this seemed rather unlikely, he suggested as an alternative the possibility of taming the world's winds:

it would be the most happy discovery that ever has happened to these northern latitudes, since in this country the N.E. winds bring frost, and the S.W. ones are attended with warmth and moisture; if the inferior currents of air could be kept perpetually from the S.W. . . . . the vegetation of this country would be doubled; as in the moist vallies of Africa, which know no frost; the number of its inhabitants would be increased, and their lives prolonged . . . (iv. 308 n.)

This blending of scientific endeavour for the improvement of man's physical state and radical political ideas for the transformation of society was well known by the 1790s. It caused men like Priestley, Darwin, and Beddoes, whom Coleridge regarded as the elect sages of the age, to be counted among the infamous 'jacobins' against whom the Church and King mobs of the age railed. Coleridge, however, took these radical hopes for a revolution in man's state and incorporated them into his description of the paradisiacal state that will prevail at the millennium. Priestley's 'pure air', produced by the decomposition of water and perhaps breathed in Beddoes' pneumatic laboratory in 1795, became the heavenly air of the millennium:

> And they, that from the chrystal river of life
> Spring up on freshen'd wing, ambrosial gales!
> The favor'd good man in his lonely walk
> Perceives them, and his silent spirit drinks
> Strange bliss which he shall recognize in heaven.
>
> (*Religious Musings*, 363–7)

At this latter day, Darwin's hopes for a transformation in the climate will also be fulfilled:

---

[16] 'Economy of Vegetation', i. 529 n.

> The THOUSAND YEARS lead up their mystic dance,
> Old OCEAN claps his hands! the DESERT shouts!
> And soft gales wafted from the haunts of Spring
> Melt the primaeval North!
>
> (ibid. 373–6)

In their inspired parody of such poetry 'The Loves of the Triangles'[17] Canning, Frere, and Ellis gave a pithy summary of the aspirations of these millenarian radicals, the philosophers of perfectibility:

> Our second principle is the *'eternal and absolute Perfectibility of Man.'* We contend, that if, as is demonstrable, we have risen from a level with the *cabbages of the field* to our present comparatively intelligent and dignified state of existence, by the mere exertion of our own *energies*; we should, if these *energies* were not repressed and subdued by the operation of prejudice, and folly, by KING-CRAFT and PRIEST-CRAFT, and the other evils incident to what is called Civilized Society, continue to exert and expand ourselves in a proportion infinitely greater than any thing of which we yet have any notion: — in a *ratio* hardly capable of being calculated by any science of which we are now masters; but which would in time raise Man from his present biped state, to a rank more worthy of his endowments and aspirations; to a rank in which he would be, as it were, *all* MIND; would enjoy unclouded perspicacity and perpetual vitality; feed on *Oxygene*, and never die, but *by his own consent*. (*Poetry of the Anti-Jacobin*, 110)

Man's need to gain knowledge to improve his general state in the world might have suggested to the philosophers that the structure of the world was in some way ill-conceived, or unsuitable for humanity. The studies of the rational Dissenters actually indicated the opposite, they believed. It was Priestley's confidence in the economy and accessibility of God's providential action in the world which first attracted him to the chemistry of airs and winds. The prodigious daily consumption of common air in respiration and combustion, and the absence of evidence to suggest that the atmosphere was less fit for life than it had ever been, convinced him that God must have made some provision in nature for making foul air wholesome once more. If this process could be found it would give direct evidence

---

[17] 'The Loves of the Triangles. A Mathematical and Philosophical Poem. Inscribed to Dr. Darwin', in *Poetry of the Anti-Jacobin* (1799), 114–29, 134–41. This volume also contains a parody of Coleridge's *Ode to the Departing Year* called 'Lines written at the close of the year 1797', and 'The Progress of Man' which is, in part, a parody of *Religious Musings*.

that the benevolent Creator sustained the very breath of man. The results of this quest for the means of the restoration of air occupied Priestley for fifteen years. He then presented the results of his work to the Royal Society in a paper which has become legendary:

I flatter myself that I have accidentally hit upon a method of restoring air which has been injured by the burning of candles, and that I have discovered at least one of the restoratives which nature employs for this purpose. It is vegetation. ('Observations on different Kinds of Air', *Phil. Trans.* lxii (1772), 166)

Priestley had 'accidentally hit upon' photosynthesis, and his modest statement is the first ever description of this fundamental process in nature. The importance of the discovery for natural philosophy was immediately seen. Priestley was awarded the Copley Medal, the Royal Society's highest accolade, and in presenting it Sir John Pringle, President of the Society, spoke lyrically of the order and benevolence Priestley had revealed:

From these discoveries we are assured, that no vegetable grows in vain, but that from the oak of the forest to the grass of the field, every individual plant is serviceable to mankind . . . In this the fragrant rose and deadly nightshade co-operate: nor is the herbage, nor the woods that flourish in the most remote and unpeopled regions unprofitable to us, nor we to them; considering how constantly the winds convey to them our vitiated air, for our relief, and for their nourishment. And if ever these salutary gales rise to storms and hurricanes, let us still trace and revere the ways of a beneficent Being; who not fortuitously but with design, nor in wrath but in mercy, thus shakes the waters and the air together, to bury in the deep those putrid and pestilential *effluvia*, which the vegetables upon the face of the earth had been insufficient to consume. (*A Discourse on the different kinds of Air* (1774), 26–7)

The idea that storms in the natural world were a purifying and necessary part of life was symbolically important to the supporters of political change. In 1794, the Dissenter Gilbert Wakefield called the political and moral tempests of the 1790s 'Dreadful, but necessary remedies, in the course of divine appointment, to rescue the ocean from stagnation, and the atmosphere from pestilence!'[18] Coleridge, in his lecture on government repression in autumn 1795, noted that

---

[18] *The Spirit of Christianity, compared with the Spirit of the Times in Great Britain* (1794), 35.

'All political controversy is at an end. Those sudden breezes and noisy gusts, which purified the atmosphere they disturbed, are hushed to deathlike silence.'[19]

Priestley's investigations into the 'science of airs' had convinced him that 'good never fails to arise out of all the evils to which, in consequence of general laws, most beneficial to the whole, it is necessarily subject'.[20] Indeed, it was an important theme of his influential *Essay on the First Principles of Government* that political systems might achieve that economy that was manifest in the natural world, and thus, as Coleridge was to put it, 'transfer the proofs of natural to moral Sciences'. Priestley wrote:

In the excellent constitution of nature, evils of all kinds, in some way or other, find their proper remedy; and when government . . . seem[s] to be in so fine a progress towards a more perfect state, is it not our wisdom to favour this progress; and to allow the remedies of all disorders to operate gradually. (*Works*, xxii. 122)

After his discoveries he expressed this optimism that the moral order would at length change by asserting that 'it does not appear impossible, but that, ultimately, one great comprehensive law shall be found to govern both the material and intellectual world.'[21]

In a footnote to 'The Economy of Vegetation' Darwin paid tribute to his friend's discoveries, among which he listed:

The restoration of vitiated air by vegetation. . . . The influence of light to enable vegetables to yield pure air. . . . The conversion by means of light of animal and vegetable substances, that would otherwise become putrid and offensive, into nourishment of vegetables. . . . The use of respiration by the blood parting with phlogiston, and imbibing dephlogisticated air. (iv. 166 n.)

This last discovery, although presented in the language of the old phlogiston chemistry, is a correct description of animal respiration. But the greatest compliment Darwin paid Priestley was in calling his poem 'The Economy of Vegetation'. This seems strikingly inappropriate for a work that devotes only 300 of its 2,440 lines to plants, yet it precisely describes the poet's belief that nature has

---

[19] *Lectures 1795*, 289.
[20] *Experiments and Observations relating to various branches of Natural Philosophy, with a continuation of the Observations on Air*, 3 vols. (1779–86), ii. 63.
[21] *Hartley's Theory of the Human Mind* (1775), p. xxv (*Works*, iii. 185).

been revealed as an orderly economic system in which, as Priestley had shown, the plant kingdom plays a crucial role.

The importance of Darwin's final canto 'Air' on the poetry of Coleridge in the years 1795–6 has been recognized since Lowes published *The Road to Xanadu*.[22] What has not been well appreciated is that Coleridge's interest in this was a result of his preoccupation with the economy of nature and society. In the descriptions of life-destroying and life-sustaining airs, Darwin had attempted to show that all imbalances in nature have natural remedies, and hence that a structure runs throughout the whole. Coleridge understood the natural economy that Darwin was portraying. In *Joan of Arc* he drew on it to show the millenarian restoration of order in France:

> A Vapor rose, pierc'd by the MAIDEN's eye.
> Guiding its course OPPRESSION sate within,
>
> . . . .
> O'er ocean westward
> The Vapor sail'd, as when a Cloud exhal'd
> From Ægypt's fields, that steam hot Pestilence,
> Travels the sky for many a trackless league,
> 'Till o'er some death-doom'd Land distant in vain
> It broods incumbent. Forthwith from the Plain
> Facing the Isle, a brighter Cloud arose
> And steer'd its course which way the Vapor went
>
> (ii. 397–8, 401–8)

The image of a pure vapour chasing a pestilential vapour, allegorizing the defeat of old corruption by the new order, is rather far-fetched outside the context of late eighteenth-century ideas on meteorology. Yet in the poem the restoration of a pure political state in France follows exactly the manner in which nature restores purity to the atmosphere. This activity Coleridge believed was millennial:

But, beware, O ye rulers of the earth! For it was ordained at the foundation of the world by the King of kings, that all corruption should conceal within its bosom that which will purify; and THEY WHO SOW PESTILENCE MUST REAP WHIRLWINDS. (*Lectures 1795*, 289)

Coleridge returned to this battle of 'pestilential winds' and 'heavenly gales' in *Religious Musings*, again using Darwin's verse. Darwin had

---

[22] Coleridge used this canto for *Joan of Arc*, ii. 402–6 and *Religious Musings*, 280–3 and n., 373–6. The best modern account of pestilential winds in Coleridge's poetry is in Piper, *Active Universe*, 89.

asserted that poisonous winds originate in volcanic eruptions, and these might at a future time erupt 'in such abundance as to contaminate the whole atmosphere, and depopulate the earth!'[23] He described one such wind, the Simoom, encountered by the explorer James Bruce in Abyssinia, and speculated that its startling appearance in the desert was caused by electric currents. Faithful to his avowal to take natural phenomena into the moral world, Coleridge used the passage of the poisonous Simoom to describe the passing of the purple-pomped Monarch. The king's existence in society, like the Simoom in nature, depends on imbalance and inequality in the world, and both bring only destruction in their passage:

> O *blest* Society!
> Fitliest depictured by some sun-scorcht waste,
> Where oft majestic thro' the tainted noon
> The SIMOOM sails, before whose purple pomp
> Who falls not prostrate dies!   (279–83)

'The Simoom is here introduced as emblematical of the pomp & powers of Despotism' Coleridge added in 1797, to remind himself.[24]

Coleridge's confidence that he could 'transfer the proofs of natural to moral Sciences' was in part founded on his knowledge of the transformations that were occurring in a society fashioned and led by those who were the leaders in natural science. After causing a revolution in the young science of electricity, Benjamin Franklin had become one of the leading figures in the foundation of the United States of America. His disciple Priestley, with brilliant experimental work in the science of airs and gases, had emerged as the leader of the reforming movement in Britain. Priestley's supporters Darwin and Beddoes were the most celebrated scientists and British radicals of the age.

Coleridge looked for the process by which this transfer of scientific insight to moral perception took place. How was it that those who had seen into the structure of nature, were also able to discover moral laws and perceive how society should be ordered? Coleridge's answer came from David Hartley's *Observations on Man*.

Hartley supposed that through the association of sense impressions in the mind, more 'complex ideas' (Locke's term) would be formed,

---

[23] 'Loves of the Plants', iv. 230 n.   [24] BL MS Ashley 408, fol. 33.

which themselves would associate to give higher and higher perceptions. He thus described a hierarchy of knowledge, from ideas
of sense (the raw material for the mind) to ideas of imagination,
ambition, self-interest, sympathy, theophany (visible presence of
God), and finally the moral sense. This ladder of attainment is of
course close to the Neoplatonic path to perfect knowledge, and, like
the Neoplatonists, Hartley believed that although all people begin
the journey, only an elect few are able to attain the highest truths.

Blending Hartley's associationism and Neoplatonism, Coleridge
described the progress of an elect being:

> And first by TERROR, Mercy's startling prelude,
> Uncharm'd the Spirit spell-bound with earthly lusts
> Till of it's nobler nature it 'gan feel
> Dim recollections; and thence soared to HOPE,
> Strong to believe whate'er of mystic good
> The ETERNAL dooms for His IMMORTAL Sons.
> From HOPE and stronger FAITH to perfect LOVE
> Attracted and absorbed: and center'd there
> GOD only to behold, and know, and feel,
> Till by exclusive Consciousness of GOD
> All self-annihilated it shall make
> GOD it's Identity: God all in all!
> We and our Father ONE!
>
> (*Religious Musings*, 39–51)

Although the lines are thoroughly Platonic in their 'dim recollections'
of a 'nobler nature', Coleridge gave three references from Hartley
in the second edition of the poem to reinforce his interpretation of
Observations on Man:

Since God is the source of all good, and consequently must at last appear
to be so, *i.e.* be associated with all our pleasures, it seems to follow, even
from this proposition, that the idea of God, and of the ways by which his
goodness and happiness are made manifest, must, at last, take place of, and
absorb all other ideas, and HE himself become, according to the language
of the scriptures, *all in all*— (*Observations on Man*, i. 114)[25]

Hartley's empirical belief that all knowledge is founded on and
derives from sense impressions implies that man's higher knowledge

[25] My references are to the edition used by Coleridge; ed. Herman Pistorius,
3 vols. (1791).

of religious and moral truths must depend on the quality of the original sense impressions. Hence *Observations on Man* is an important essay on the correspondence between the natural and moral world, for it shows how the impressions of nature can influence an individual's progress as a moral being. It follows from Hartley that those who have studied the natural world most closely, and have seen its economy, will have progressed further and have more developed faculties than the rest of mankind. Hence they will qualify for the status of 'elect beings'.

The idea of perfectibility in *Observations on Man* was strictly limited to the development of individuals. However, in his abridgement *Hartley's Theory of the Human Mind on the principle of the Association of Ideas* (1775), Priestley changed the theory significantly in a concluding chapter 'On the practical Application of the Doctrine of Necessity' which he wrote himself but did not admit.[26] In this chapter Priestley applied the associationist process to the entire history of mankind and anticipated the advent of a new type of human beings who would 'approach to the paradisaical state, in which our first parents, though naked, were not ashamed'.[27] Elsewhere Priestley made it clear that he believed the natural philosophers to be an elect group, for they alone had studied nature closely enough to acquire millennial characteristics. In *The History and Present State of Electricity* he had written:

A PHILOSOPHER ought to be something greater, and better than another man. The contemplation of the works of God should give a sublimity to his virtue, should expand his benevolence, extinguish every thing mean, base, and selfish in his nature, give a dignity to all his sentiments, and teach him to aspire to the moral perfections of the great author of all things. What great and exalted beings would philosophers be, would they but let the objects about which they are conversant have their proper moral effect upon their minds! (p. xx)

Erasmus Darwin was another believer in the progressiveness of creatures through the effect of the natural world. Like Priestley he

---

[26] pp. 365–7. This was first pointed out by R. B. Hatch, 'Joseph Priestley: An Addition to Hartley's *Observations*', *JHI* xxxvi (1975), 548–50. The clearest exposition of Hartley's attitude towards perfectibility is M. Leslie, 'Mysticism Misunderstood: David Hartley and the Idea of Progress', *JHI* xxxiii (1972), 625–32.

[27] *Hartley's Theory*, 367.

extended Hartley's associationism to the progressive course of nature as a whole:

> from their first rudiment, or primordium, to the termination of their lives, all animals undergo perpetual transformations; which are in part produced by . . . associations; and many of these acquired forms or propensities are transmitted to their posterity. This idea is analogous to the improving excellence observable in every part of the creation; such as in the progressive increase of the . . . wisdom and happiness of its inhabitants. (*Zoonomia; or, The Laws of Organic Life*, i (1794), 502–3)

These 'evolutionary' perceptions of nature supported Coleridge's belief that man is progressing to greater social and moral perfection. In the first lecture on revealed religion in March 1795 he said: 'From the whole circle of Nature we collect Proofs that the Omnipotent operates in a process from the Slip to the full-blown Rose, from the embryo to the full-grown Man how vast & various the Changes!'[28]

With a clear idea of the elect band of philosophers who were to carry the principles of ancient knowledge forward into the modern world, Coleridge now had the idea of how this transformation of society was to be achieved by the 'transfer of natural to moral sciences'. All his hopes rested on the band of 'patriot sages', the young scientists who had followed the work of Newton, Franklin, and Priestley. Wise through long and careful study of the natural world, they had come to know its inner order. By mental association, the sense impressions thus gained would be transformed into moral perceptions, and these elect beings would then be prepared as the social engineers of the age. In the final lecture on revealed religion Coleridge tried to illustrate the associative process:

> In the country, the Love and Power of the great Invisible are everywhere perspicuous, and by degrees we become partakers of that which we are accustomed to contemplate. The Beautiful and the Good are miniatured on the Heart of the Contemplator as the surrounding Landscape on a Convex Mirror. (*Lectures 1795*, 224)

Through the development of the moral sense, the elect band will come to have perfect knowledge of the moral order, and thus power over their own societies.

But the events of the 1790s taught Coleridge the price to be paid for this 'Revolution of Souls'. The kings of the earth who had leagued

---

[28] *Lectures 1795*, 108–9.

with Mystery still reigned. Yet fall they must, for the Whore of
Babylon had been defeated by the natural philosophers:

> For She hath fallen
> On whose black front was written MYSTERY;
> She that reel'd heavily, whose wine was blood;
> She that worked whoredom with the DAEMON POWER,
> And from the dark embrace all evil things
> Brought forth and nurtured . . .
>
> *(Religious Musings, 342–7)*

Years of social inequality and injustice in Europe had caused an
accumulation of wrongs, and it was the uncontrolled release of these
forces during the French Revolution that produced the storm that had
swept through that country. By 1796 Coleridge was disillusioned with
the French leadership for flagrantly failing to mould a better State
from the energies that the revolution had released. Yet he still expected,
even hoped for, revolutions in the other European States, including
England, and was confident that in England there were social leaders
with the insight and power to mould a better order of society.

As a model of successful revolution Coleridge took Franklin's work
in the American struggle for independence. The philosopher who
had tamed natural storms was the paradigm for those who must
transfer their wisdom to the moral order. In *Religious Musings* the
pointed rod of the lightning conductor which 'threw off' electric fluid
to tame the storm, was transformed into the writing quill of the elect
sage, emitting from its tip the calming fluid of truth:

> Warriors, and Lords, and Priests—all the sore ills
> That vex and desolate our mortal life.
> Wide-wasting ills! yet each th'immediate source
> Of mightier good. Their keen necessities
> To ceaseless action goading human thought
> Have made Earth's reasoning animal her Lord;
> And the pale-featured Sage's trembling hand
> Strong as an host of arméd Deities!   (229–36)

He portrayed the calm before the political storm that was to burst
on England in *The Plot Discovered*: 'Every town is insulated: the
vast conductors are destroyed by the which the electric fluid of truth
was conveyed from man to man, and nation to nation.'[29]

---

[29] *Lectures 1795*, 313.

Religious Musings actually incorporates the history of the final millennium of the world which Coleridge was pondering as he published it. Like the imbalance of electrical fluid in the heavens, the accumulated imbalance of moral forces is to be released in a purging tempest that will bring about a social revolution. The storm will be precipitated by 'eloquent men', the energetic leaders of the popular radical movement who have 'waken'd' the lower classes to the possibility of social change. But such men are not members of the elect band, for they have no knowledge of the inner structure of the world. Borrowing from Pope, Coleridge saw the elect band then spreading outwards like the ripples on a lake:

> O'er waken'd realms Philosophers and Bards
> Spread in concentric circles: they whose souls
> Conscious of their high dignities from God,
> Brook not Wealth's rivalry; and they who long
> Enamoured with the charms of order hate
> Th'unseemly disproportion . . .   (239–44)

In a lecture on religion, he had described the same process at work in the teaching of Christ: 'Universal Equality is the object of the Mess[iah's] mission not to be procured by the tumultuous uprising of an indignant multitude but this final result of an unresisting yet deeply principled Minority, which gradually absorbing kindred minds shall at last become the whole.'[30]

The experiences of the French sages, like the chemist Lavoisier, guillotined because 'the republic has no need of *savants*', troubled Coleridge. In *A Moral and Political Lecture* he declared:

The annals of the French Revolution have recorded in Letters of Blood, that the Knowledge of the Few cannot counteract the Ignorance of the Many; that the Light of Philosophy, when it is confined to a small Minority, points out the Possessors as the Victims, rather than the Illuminators, of the Multitude. (*Lectures 1795*, 6)

The urgency of the situation seemed to tell against patient methods, and in the notebook he considered sowing 'Political wisdom . . . by the broad-cast, not dibble'.[31] The elect band of natural philosophers must be ready for the storm. It would break any day:

---

[30] Ibid. 218.   [31] CN i. 116.

These on the fated day,
. . . hush'd awhile with patient eye serene
Shall watch the mad careering of the storm;
Then o'er the wild and wavy chaos rush
And tame the outrageous mass, with plastic might
Moulding Confusion to such perfect forms,
As erst were wont, bright visions of the day!   (252–61)

In this last age of the world, chaos will again return, as in the beginning of Creation. And from that primeval state natural philosophers and sages of the new order will work to create the revitalized millennial world. As agents of the plastic power of God they will mould chaos to bring about the age yet only dreamed of.

5

Nature and the Language of God

The study and contemplation of the works of creation, and of
the power and wisdom of God revealed and manifested in those
works, made a great part of the religious devotion of the times
in which they were written; and it was this . . . that led to the
discovery of the principles upon which, what are now called
Sciences, are established . . .

Paine, The Age of Reason

WHEN Coleridge travelled north in January 1796 to recruit sub-
scribers for *The Watchman*, and perhaps to gauge the mood of the
radical provincial leaders for revolution, he stopped at Derby to pay
a call on Erasmus Darwin. The meeting seems to have disappointed
him:

Dr. Darwin would have been ashamed to have rejected Hutton's theory of
the earth without having minutely examined it; yet what is it to us *how* the
earth was made, a thing impossible to be known, and useless if known?
This system the doctor did not reject without having severely studied it; but
all at once he makes up his mind on such important subjects, as whether
we be the outcasts of a blind idiot called Nature, or the children of an all-
wise and infinitely good God . . . (Letter to Josiah Wade, 27 January 1796;
CL i. 177)

He was referring to James Hutton's newly published work *Theory
of the Earth*,[1] which is now honoured as one of the founding essays
in the science of geology. Coleridge and Darwin evidently had
discussed the work, whose author was an old friend of the Lunar
Society, and rather surprisingly Coleridge thought that Darwin
had rejected the theory. Coleridge certainly had: it was, he said,
unprovable, and moreover, of no use: 'what is it to us *how* the earth
was made, a thing impossible to be known, and useless if known?'
James Hutton's *Theory of the Earth* is a paradigm essay in
Newton's empirical method. Attacking earlier attempts to explain
the origins of the earth for the introducing of unnecessary events such
as universal floods (the 'neptunists') or fires (the 'vulcanists'), and

---

[1] *Theory of the Earth, with Proofs and Illustrations*, 2 vols. (1795).

irrelevant causes such as divine retribution, Hutton allowed only present-day forces to account for changes in the earth's surface. Thus Coleridge was quite wrong to claim that the theory is unprovable, for Hutton's only assumption is merely inductive: that the order of nature remains constant. The geologist found sufficient power from the forces of wind, water, pressure, and fire, to account for the unending pattern of formation and destruction of land-masses, and so endorsed Newton's principle that 'to the same effects, we must as far as possible, assign the same causes'.

Coleridge's other objection to the theory, that it was 'useless', is more interesting, for it sheds light on his early attitude to scientific endeavour. Although a philosopher of the breadth and depth of Coleridge might be thought to have searched after knowledge for its own sake, of the multitude of references to eighteenth-century science in his lectures, poems, and notes before 1798, not one merely notes a phenomenon as a neutral fact of the universe. All had some use for him. The present example is no exception. Coleridge would have been aware that, if true, Hutton's theory was an argument in favour of an eternal and self-sustaining world, with the forces of creation and destruction equally balanced:

> When we trace the parts of which this terrestrial system is composed, and when we view the general connection of those several parts, the whole presents a machine of a peculiar construction by which it is adapted to a certain end. We perceive a fabric, erected in wisdom, to obtain a purpose worthy of the power that is apparent in the production of it. (*Theory of the Earth*, i. 3)

This is deism: the universe is the creation of a supreme Being, but that being is no longer involved in his world. 'I was told, that Hutton was an atheist,' Coleridge gossiped in a letter to John Thelwall in June 1796, '& procured his three massy Quartos on the principles of Knowledge in the hopes of finding some arguments in favor of atheism—but lo! I discovered him to be a profoundly pious Deist'.[2]

Thus it is deism that is the root of Coleridge's disagreement with Darwin. If Hutton's *Theory of the Earth* were true it could be that we were 'outcasts of a blind idiot called Nature'. Hence, for a defender of revealed religion such as Coleridge, this theory was not simply 'useless', but actually damaging to his theistic beliefs. Indeed

[2] *CL* i. 222.

it was for exactly this reason that Coleridge had attacked Newton's doctrine of aether in the footnote to *Joan of Arc*, aiming not principally to undermine the scientific validity of the aether hypothesis, but to attack its deistic consequences.

Newton, Hutton, and Darwin all held different theistic beliefs, but they were each capable of evaluating a scientific theory on its ability to account for evidence presented in support. A telling example is Darwin's acceptance in 1789, the year of its publication, of the new chemical system of Lavoisier which threw out the old phlogiston chemistry of his friends in the Lunar Society. Darwin's impartiality was not shared by Coleridge, and because of this he remains the antithesis of the disinterested inquirer into nature, however great his interest in natural phenomena. For Coleridge, it was not the truth of a particular theory but its usefulness in supporting his beliefs and contributing to his own work that was his criterion for accepting it. Moreover, because all the natural phenomena noted by Coleridge have a use, and are employed in his writing to support and illustrate ideas, they may be said to constitute parts of a language of nature whose meaning is to be elucidated by the use to which such descriptions can be put.

The notion of nature as the language of God was not unique to Coleridge. James Thomson and Mark Akenside had written about it in the eighteenth century, and this passage from Akenside's *The Pleasures of Imagination* (1744) is typical of their work:

> some within a finer mould
> She wrought, and temper'd with a purer flame.
> To these the sire omnipotent unfolds
> The world's harmonious volume, there to read
> The transcript of himself. On every part
> They trace the bright impressions of his hand:
> In earth or air, the meadow's purple stores,
> The moon's mild radiance, or the virgin's form
> Blooming with rosy smiles, they see portray'd
> That uncreated beauty, which delights
> The mind supreme.   (i. 97–107)

However, the earlier poets do not develop their theme. It is enough for Akenside that the language of God consists of one word, 'Beauty'; for, apparently, that is all that those of 'finer mould' wish to read there. Coleridge quoted this passage in his first lecture on religion. He, however, was not content to keep the notion of a natural language of God merely at the level of pious metaphor, and embarked instead upon 'abstruser Reasonings unentertaining indeed but necessary'.[3] When he referred to nature as God's language he made clear that he meant it literally: 'We see our God everywhere,' he wrote later in the year; 'the Universe in the most literal Sense is his written Language.'[4] This more rigorous approach did not, of course, prevent him from writing poetry on the language of God in nature which is as fine as any:

> But *thou*, my babe! shalt wander like a breeze
> By lakes and sandy shores, beneath the crags
> Of ancient mountain, and beneath the clouds,
> Which image in their bulk both lakes and shores
> And mountain crags: so shalt thou see and hear
> The lovely shapes and sounds intelligible
> Of that eternal language, which thy God
> Utters, who from eternity doth teach
> Himself in all, and all things in himself.
> Great universal Teacher!
>
> ('Frost at Midnight', 54–63)

Coleridge's interest in the relationship of nature and language may originate in his reading of David Hartley who had discussed the origins of language in *Observations on Man*, and favoured the view that language began when God gave simple speech to Adam and Eve for them to name the animals in Eden. After the Fall this language became corrupted as men learned the names of evil things, and used language to promote self-interest. The confusion of tongues at the tower of Babel, Hartley argued, was caused by God to prevent this original and powerful language becoming too corrupted and thus dominating mankind through false perceptions. Adam's original tongue had been a complete and natural system, fully able to express all conceptions without ambiguity. Thus as the expansion of knowledge in the eighteenth century brought mankind closer to an original state of pure knowledge, Hartley saw the need to return to the original language and through an integration of the world's tongues to restore the original state of natural speech:

If all the simple articulate sounds, with all the radical words, which are found in the present languages, were appropriated to objects and ideas agreeable

---

[3] *Lectures 1795*, 95.   [4] Ibid. 339

to the present senses of words, and their fitness to represent objects and ideas, so as to make all consistent with itself; if, farther, the best rules of etymology and syntax were selected from the present languages, and applied to the radical words here spoken of, so as to render them capable of expressing all the variations in objects and ideas, as far as possible, *i.e.* so as to grow proportionably to the growth of knowledge, this might also be termed a philosophical language . . . (*Observations on Man*, i. 316–17)

Hartley believed Hebrew was the language most closely related to God's original gift, and he suggested that by sifting through the dispersed ancient tongues, the pristine language might be pieced together. Thus he anticipated the millennial age when the structure of the natural world would be mirrored by man's natural language.

Priestley published *Hartley's Theory of the Human Mind* in 1775, and in the Introduction suggested that the 'simple and general laws' that had been discovered to govern the universe, such as Newton's laws of motions, or his own law of electrical attraction, could be thought of as 'a short alphabet', from which the world's language might be generated as a precise scientific code. Priestley saw no reason why, once the facts of the universe had been elucidated, a language of nature should not become apparent to men. When the natural philosophers had completed their work, and the structure of the heavens had been made plain, God would suddenly be revealed speaking directly to mankind through nature, as he had been doing since the beginning of time. At this moment the natural and social world would mirror each other, and the golden age would return.

These early attempts to elucidate the relation between language and mankind's perception of nature caught Coleridge's interest. In *Observations on Man* Hartley had speculated whether mental images (ideas) could become so vivid that they were mistaken for impressions of the world. On the flyleaf to his copy Coleridge wrote: 'Ideas may become as vivid & distinct, & the feelings accompanying them as vivid, as original Impressions — and this may finally make a man independent of his Senses. — one use of poetry.'[5] Poetry might create such powerful images inside the mind of the reader that ideas could replace sense impressions completely. Hence people would be led away from their false perceptions of nature to the true picture created by the poet's words.

[5] BL c. 126. 1. 2.

If this was to be the power of the poet, he had to know that the language he was using was indeed the philosophical language Hartley had called for, faithfully mirroring the language of nature. This striving for a correct language to name reality is apparent in *Religious Musings* where the poet refers not to qualities of the world, but to the names of those qualities:

> There is one Mind, one omnipresent Mind,
> Omnific. His most holy name is LOVE   (114–5).
>
>   She hath fallen
> On whose black front was written MYSTERY   (342–3).

As the true language works on the imagination and strong impressions are formed, old perceptions and unrealities disappear from men's minds:

> Thus from the Elect, regenerate through faith.
> Pass the dark Passions and what thirsty Cares
> Drink up the spirit, and the dim regards
> Self center. Lo they vanish! or acquire
> New names, new features—by supernal grace
> Enrobed with Light, and naturaliz'd in Heaven.   (97–102)

Yet if nature was God's language, it had to be saying something of significance. It was not enough merely to be pointing to God's presence in nature. Nature as a language thus differs significantly from nature as evidence of design (the teleological argument), for this seeks no more than to establish intelligent design in the order of the universe and thus prove God's existence. To prove that nature is a language, it is necessary to show that there is purpose in the design and that this can be communicated to man. Philosophically, this has proved a very difficult task. In this passage from the first lecture on religion Coleridge argues for purpose in the structure, yet his argument is no more than a restatement of the argument for design:

No one . . . that knows the principles of optics and the structure of the eye can believe that it was formed without skill in that Science, or that the Ear was formed without knowledge of Sounds, or that the male and female in animals were not formed for each other and for continuing the Species. (*Lectures 1795*, 93)

The lecturer says that the purpose of the eye is to see, and the purpose of the ear is to hear. This looks as if it is evidence for design,

although the passage can be rewritten to imply nothing of the sort:
'the function of the eye is seeing; the function of the ear is hearing;
the function of sexual division is sexual reproduction.' Coleridge
presents no *reason* for sight or hearing or for propagation, for none
of these skills means anything other than what it is. If Nature is to
communicate as a language, it has to be purposeful, and humans
have to perceive why nature is structured the way it is. What is the
point of all this design? Is it merely so that we can use our perceptive
faculties, appreciate the design of the system, and applaud the deity
on his handiwork?

The Omnipotent has unfolded to us the Volume of the World, that there
we may read the Transcript of himself. In Earth or Air the meadow's
purple stores, the Moons mild radiance, or the Virgins form Blooming with
rosy smiles, we see pourtrayed the bright Impressions of the eternal Mind.
(ibid. 94)

—to the pious man all Nature is . . . beautiful because its every Feature
is the Symbol and all its Parts the written Language of infinite Goodness
and all powerful Intelligence. (ibid. 158)

The danger with such reasoning is not so much that the deity begins
to look rather self-satisfied and self-glorifying, but that it needs only
one example to undermine it. If the natural philosophers were to
discover that part of the world was less than perfect—if, for example,
they had concluded that mankind really would have been better off
with harder bones—they would necessarily deduce that the deity was
not an 'all powerful Intelligence', or not omnibenevolent. Coleridge's
argument, as he came to realize, is vulnerable to the existence in the
world of evil.

Coleridge seems to argue that the statement 'Nature is harmonious'
is true a posteriori, through observation of how the world is. Thus,
by assuming that nature is God's language, he deduces that God is
a perfect being. In fact, like most of his age, his argument is a-priori:
God is by definition a perfect being; nature is God's language (by
assumption); thus nature is harmonious (by deduction). He would
not however have admitted this. In a lecture on religion Coleridge
praised Newton for his empirical approach to the assertion 'nature
is harmonious':

Ptolemy and Descartes exerted their Fancies and conceptions to find out
how the World ought to have been made, and having satisfied themselves
in this point they concluded that the World was so made, and a curious

World they made of it. Sir Isaac Newton employed his patient Industry and lynx-eyed Penetration in discovering how the World had been constituted and having in part developed it he was soon able to prove that as it was made, so it ought to have been! (ibid. 189)

Yet the moment he came across Newton's aether hypothesis, which, though founded on the empirical method, seemed to deny God's action in nature, Coleridge simply denounced it:

For if matter by any powers or properties *given* to it, can produce the order of the visible world, and even generate thought, why may it not have possessed such properties by *inherent* right? and where is the necessity of a God? (*Joan of Arc*, ii. 34 n.)

If nature was functioning as a language for mankind and was understood, it had to affect behaviour in some way. In *Joan of Arc* Coleridge evoked Plato's Cave image to show how nature taught man to progress to a vision of God:

> him First, him Last to view
> Thro' meaner powers and secondary things
> Effulgent, as thro' clouds that veil his blaze.
> For all that meets the bodily sense I deem
> Symbolical, one mighty alphabet
> For infant minds; and we in this low world
> Placed with our backs to bright Reality,
> That we may learn with young unwounded ken
> Things from their shadows.   (ii. 16–24)

The Cave image in book VII of *The Republic* portrayed men, shackled since childhood with their faces to the back of a cave, believing that the shadows and reflected sounds they perceived were aspects of the real world. Plato believed the world we perceive is a veil which hides the reality of things from us. Coleridge, though, interpreted the allegory differently, for nature seemed to him to communicate through an alphabet of simple sense impressions. Speaking through the natural world, God teaches mankind how to progress through nature's hierarchy of levels towards the divine source. In *Religious Musings* the 'elect of heaven' are seen climbing this didactic ladder of nature, 'Treading beneath their feet all visible things / As steps, that upward to their Father's Throne / Lead gradual'.[6] Coleridge reinforced the path of ascent through a Platonic chain of being in his lectures:

From the whole circle of Nature we collect Proofs that the Omnipotent operates in a process from the Slip to the full-blown Rose, from the embryo to the full-grown Man how vast & various the Changes! (*Lectures 1795*, 108–9)

the mind must enlarge its sphere of activity, and progressive by nature, must never rest content. . . . fixing our eyes on the glittering Summits that rise one above the other in Alpine endlessness . . . [it] urges us up the ascent of Being, amusing the ruggedness of the road by the beauty and wonder of the ever-widening Prospect. (ibid. 337–8)

If there is a clear message of progression in the natural world which shows mankind how to develop, this could not conflict with biblical revelation or prophecies which predict through revealed knowledge the progressiveness of creation:

Quare—might not a Commentary on the Revelations be written from late philosophical discoveries? (*CN* i. 133)

Indeed, Coleridge saw no difficulty in using the language of nature to explain or clarify biblical language. Calling on eighteenth-century research to aid what was commonly thought to be an absurd biblical story, he wrote: 'Jonas—a monodrama— *Vide* Hunter's Anatomy of a Whale'.[7] He was referring to John Hunter's paper to the Royal Society 'Observations on the Structure and Oeconomy of *Whales*',[8] evidently intending to show the physical possibility of the events described in the Book of Jonah.

In the discussion of prophecy in the third lecture on religion 'Sir Isaac Newton and John Locke and David Hartley' are evoked to show that there is order and 'Procession' in nature, and that biblical prophecies are more than mere accidental guesses.[9] Elsewhere biblical revelation is compared to a magnifying glass, which assists 'without contradicting our natural vision'.[10] Revealed religion and natural phenomena were created by God, and a contradiction between the two languages would have been a self-contradiction within the divine being.

It was natural phenomena, rather than revealed religion, that remained foremost in Coleridge's mind at this time. In his notebook

---

[6] ll. 57–9.   [7] *CN* i. 32.   [8] *Phil. Trans.* lxxvii (1787), 371–450.
[9] *Lectures 1795*, 150.   [10] Ibid. 91.

he wrote: 'Reason the Sun—Revelation the comet which feeds it'.[11] Such an emphasis suggests that he was influenced by Thomas Paine's much-abused work *The Age of Reason* (1793 and 1795), in which traditional arguments for deism are revived in a forceful defence of natural religion:

THE WORD OF GOD IS THE CREATION WE BEHOLD: And it is in *this word* . . . that God speaketh universally to man. . . . It is only in the CREATION that all our ideas and conceptions of a *word of God* can unite. The creation speaketh an universal language, independently of human speech or human language, multiplied and various as they be. It is an ever existing original, which every man can read. (*The Age of Reason*, i. 26–7)

Paine, notoriously, found in nature a more coherent language of the deity than in the books of the Bible. Commenting on Jeremiah's prophecies, Paine wrote: 'Were I, or any other man, to write in such a disordered manner, no body would read what was written; and every body would suppose, that the writer was in a state of insanity.'[12]

Coleridge criticized the theological weaknesses of *The Age of Reason* in his third lecture on religion, but seriously misrepresented Paine, who, he said, had found the universe to be a 'chaos of Unintelligibles'.[13] This 'misunderstanding' seems to have been deliberate, caused by Coleridge's need to distance himself from philosophers such as Godwin, Paine, and Newton, of whom he disapproved, yet from whom he gained much. Paine was actually a greater supporter of natural religion than Priestley, who reviewed *The Age of Reason* in 1794:

Mr. Paine calls to his aid the marks of *benevolence* which are impressed on the face of nature, supposing the author of it to say to man, 'Learn from my munificence to all, to be kind to each other.' There are, no doubt, marks of benevolence, as well as of power, in the constitution of nature and the conduct of Providence, sufficient to enable a reflecting mind to conclude that the Author of nature is supremely benevolent, and that the great end of all his works is the happiness of his creatures. But this is not so *apparent*, but that many have been drawn a contrary conclusion; and there are appearances in nature which would seem to justify the generality of mankind, who are unable to take enlarged and extensive views of things, in drawing it. (*A Continuation of the Letters to the Philosophers and Politicians of France* (etc.); *Works*, xxi. 129–30)

---

[11] *CN* i. 88.   [12] *Age of Reason*, ii. 52.   [13] *Lectures 1795*, 150.

That year Coleridge made notes for a 'Sermon on Faith' and asserted 'The superiority of the knowledge which we have by faith to the knowledge which we have by Natural Philosophy'.[14] Yet after reading Paine revelation is brought to the support of reason, not vice versa; and Coleridge's lectures on revealed religion are filled with natural theology, despite seeing in *The Age of Reason* his beloved Isaiah dismissed as 'incoherent, bombastical rant', Ecclesiastes as 'the solitary reflections of a worn-out debauchee', and the whole Bible as 'a history of wickedness'.

In the Bristol lectures of 1795 Coleridge denied the two central dogmas of the Christian faith: Trinitarian Godhead and the deity of Jesus Christ. He emphasized instead the teachings of Christ, whom he referred to as the 'inspired Philanthropist of Galilee', and stressed that Christ had existed in a peculiar relationship to the deity to reveal his word through his ministry of teaching and healing, and eventually through his death. But orthodox Christians believe not merely that Christ heard and taught the word of God, but that he was the Word of God, the *logos* or second person of the Trinity. For the Church Christ does not need to teach or act to show men what God intends for mankind, as his very existence reveals it.

Coleridge's emphasis at this time on nature as the language of God seems to have been necessary to add to his Unitarian beliefs. Natural theology avoided the charge of deism which could otherwise have been made: that without Christ as the *logos*, the unitarian God was remote and unconcerned about the fate of his creation. 'We see our God everywhere—the Universe in the most literal Sense in his written Language', he stressed.[15] Were this not so, Coleridge would have had no more to support his faith than the reported word of God, transmitted through his elect band of prophets.

When Coleridge looked to nature for a clear sign of God's literal presence, he inevitably chose the sun, the source of all life in the heavens. At the centre of the order and economy of nature that had been revealed by the natural philosophers, the sun was an apt signifier of the deity. In an early draft of *The Destiny of Nations* Coleridge attempted to rewrite the Athanasian Creed for the natural theologian: 'God in God immanent, the eternal Word, / That gives forth, yet

---

[14] CN i. 6.   [15] *Lectures 1795*, 339.

remains—Sun, that at once / Dawns, rises, sets and crowns the Height of Heaven'.[16]

The complexity of Coleridge's early thought on the correspondence between the Son of God and the sun of nature, is evident in the opening of *Religious Musings*. The poem begins with a simple meditation on the dawn of the first Christmas:

> THIS is the time, when most divine to hear,
> As with a Cherub's 'loud uplifted' trump
> The voice of Adoration my thrill'd heart
> Rouses! And with the rushing noise of wings
> Transports my spirit to the favor'd fields
> Of Bethlehem, there in shepherd's guise to sit
> Sublime of extacy, and mark entranc'd
> The glory-streaming VISION throng the night.   (1–8)

The reader is lulled by this conventional opening as the poet in the traditional guise of the shepherd high above Bethlehem, watches nature unfold on the dawn of the first Christmas morning. The angelic host is presented as the system of heavenly planets, revolving in their glory. It is a standard image, which Milton also uses:

> Ah not more radiant, nor loud harmonies
> Hymning more unimaginably sweet
> With choral songs around th'ETERNAL MIND,
> The constellated company of WORLDS
> Danc'd jubilant . . .
>
> (*Religious Musings*, 9–13)

> Such music (as 'tis said)
> Before was never made,
>   But when of old the sons of morning sung,
> While the creator great
> His constellations set . . .
>
> (Milton, 'On the Morning of Christ's Nativity', 117–21)

It thus comes as a shock to realize that the poet of *Religious Musings* is not celebrating the birth of Christ, but the rising sun itself:

> what time the startling East
> Saw from her dark womb leap her flamy Child!
> Glory to God in the Highest! PEACE on Earth!   (13–15)

---

[16] *Complete Poetical Works of Coleridge*, ii. 1025.

The self-revealing God, whose will is most clearly manifest in nature, is now present in the gift of the sun, for as the centre and fountain of all life the sun is the clearest manifestation of the intentions of the deity for his world.

Coleridge's preoccupation with the economic and cyclical system of the world is the subject of the later chapters of this study. Throughout it Coleridge will be seen trying to answer the question he had debated with Erasmus Darwin that winter afternoon in 1796: are we 'the outcasts of a blind idiot called Nature?' If, as Coleridge passionately believed, the truths of nature were rapidly being revealed by the natural philosophers, and nature was shown to be a particularly 'economic' system, what was that telling man about his own state and future being? What sense could mankind make of the economy of nature?

6

Religious Musings:
'A Desultory Poem'?

WHEN Coleridge died in 1834 the most widely read appreciation
of his work was written by William Lisle Bowles, an early hero of
the dead sage.[1] Commenting on *Religious Musings*, the epic poem
of Coleridge's twenty-third year, Bowles called it 'by far the most
correct, sublime, chaste, and beautiful of his poems'. If the review
could have reached Coleridge, he is unlikely to have agreed. It is
true that on its publication in his first collection, *Poems on Various
Subjects*, in April 1796 he had rested 'all my poetical credit' on
Religious Musings,[2] and it had enjoyed warm praise from, among
others, Charles Lamb and Wordsworth.[3] Yet within a year Coleridge
was calling his poem 'obscure', evidently giving way to those critics
who had found it too difficult.[4] In later years he always tended to
dismiss it as a youthful indulgence in metaphysics and theology,
neither of which were too well grounded in his thought at the time
of its composition. Since Coleridge's death, literary fashion has
generally agreed with its author's later assessment, and not with

---

[1] W. L. Bowles, 'Coleridge a Private Soldier', *Athenaeum*, cccliii (August, 1834),
613; reprinted in R. and J. Haven and M. Adams (eds.), *Samuel Taylor Coleridge:
An Annotated Bibliography of Criticism and Scholarship*, i: 1793–1899 (London,
1976), 80.

[2] 'I rest for all my poetical credit on the *Religious Musings*', Coleridge wrote to
Benjamin Flower on 1 Apr. 1796; he repeated the assertion in letters to Thomas Poole
and John Thelwall of the same month (*CL* i. 197, 203, 205).

[3] See *CL* i. 215–6. It is possible that Wordsworth wrote directly to Coleridge; see
R. Woof, 'Wordsworth and Coleridge: Some Early Matters', in J. Wordsworth (ed.),
Bicentenary Wordsworth Studies in Memory of John Alban Finch (Ithaca, NY, 1970),
82–3. Wordsworth praised ll. 364–75 and 403–28, which because of misnumbering
in the first edition are often wrongly identified. They are 'Such delights / As float
to earth, permitted visitants!' to 'Strange bliss which he shall recognize in heaven'
and 'O Years! the blest preeminence of Saints!' to 'Wraps in one blaze earth, heaven,
and deepest hell.' For Charles Lamb's eulogistic praise of the poem see *The Letters
of Charles and Mary Ann Lamb*, ed. E. W. Marrs, jun., 3 vols. (Ithaca, NY and
London, 1975–), i. 11, 28, 95.

[4] Coleridge acknowledged that the poem had been judged to be 'obscure' in a
letter to Cottle of Feb. 1797 (*CL* i. 309).

Bowles. Whereas a century ago an anthology of romantic poetry would almost certainly have included *Religious Musings*, it is now displaced by its contemporaneous 'conversation poems', and critics will dismiss it as 'Miltonic'.

Religious Musings is subtitled 'A Desultory Poem, Written On Christmas' Eve, In The Year Of Our Lord, 1794'. Without doubt Coleridge began to write it about then, for he mentions a poem (which for a year he called 'The Nativity') in a letter to Robert Southey of 31 December 1794.[5] But Coleridge did not finish this poem until his collection of poetry was almost completely set by Nathaniel Biggs in Bristol, fifteen months later. Indeed, some of the political events *Religious Musings* discusses did not occur until late in 1795. If not a great or an integrated poem, it was a working draft of Coleridge's thoughts during an exceptionally important year of his life. For the subject of *Religious Musings* is quite simply the entire history of the world.

1. Introduction (1–15)

The opening scene is set at the beginning of the modern age, with the poet introduced as a modern prophet and sage 'in the Spirit', like the great prophet of the Apocalypse St John of Patmos. The quotation from Milton's 'At the Solemn Music', and clear borrowings from Milton's Christmas poetry, 'On the Morning of Christ's Nativity' and 'The Passion', sets the mood of conventional homage:

> THIS is the time, when most divine to hear,
> As with a Cherub's 'loud uplifted' trump
> The voice of Adoration my thrill'd heart
> Rouses! And with the rushing noise of wings
> Transports my spirit to the favor'd fields
> Of Bethlehem, there in shepherd's guise to sit
> Sublime of extacy, and mark entranc'd
> The glory-streaming VISION throng the night   (1–8)

Coleridge then launches his poem into heterodox theology. Because he denies traditional Christian teaching on the nature of God and Christ, he cannot carry on the pretence of a Christmas hymn. Instead,

---

[5] 'The Poem is in blank Verse on the Nativity', Coleridge wrote to Southey on 29 Dec. 1794 (*CL* i. 147). The formal date of composition (24 Dec.) was the day on which Coleridge wrote to end his relationship with Mary Evans. See Fruman, *Coleridge*, 3–12 for the significance of Coleridge's own dating of the poems.

he substitutes the rising sun for the Son of Man, and the Newtonian system of planets heralds the birth:

> Ah not more radiant, nor loud harmonies
> Hymning more unimaginably sweet
> With choral songs around th'ETERNAL MIND,
> The constellated company of WORLDS
> Danc'd jubilant: what time the startling East
> Saw from her dark womb leap her flamy Child!
> Glory to God in the Highest! PEACE on Earth!   (9–15)

2. Person of Christ (16–27a)

Rightly embarrassed by this tongue-in-cheek opening, Coleridge immediately tries to make amends by explaining his Unitarian understanding of Christ's uniqueness. Christ was not a 'God Man', as traditional Christology taught, but a 'Good Man', so perfectly human that he acted as a kind of window to the deity, or, in the poet's own imagery, a metaphysical prism which, instead of splitting white light into its component colours, splits the unintelligible unity into a component trinity of Power, Wisdom, and Love. The image, a good one, is Neoplatonic:

> Yet Thou more bright than all that Angel Blaze,
> Despised GALILÆAN! Man of Woes!
> For chiefly in the oppressed Good Man's face
> The Great Invisible (by symbols seen)
> Shines with peculiar and concentred light,
>
>   .   .   .   .   .
>
> Who thee beheld thy imag'd Father saw.
> His Power and Wisdom from thy awful eye
> Blended their beams, and loftier Love sate there   (16–26)

3. His Prayer on the Cross (27b–33)

Coleridge was a devotee of Priestley's materialist metaphysics at the time he wrote this section of the poem, and so cannot allow Christ any immaterial substance, such as a soul, human or divine, to outlive the death of his body. What survives at the crucifixion was Christ's example and his teaching, the summation of which was his prayer from the Cross 'Father, forgive them; for they know what they do.'[6] This is the shortest section of the poem, and Coleridge rather

---

[6] Luke 23: 34.

curiously inverts the Gospel account: at the death of Christ there
was darkness throughout the land, and the tombs of the dead opened:

> When thy insulted Anguish wing'd the prayer
> Harp'd by Archangels, when they sing of Mercy!
> Which when th'ALMIGHTY heard, from forth his Throne
> Diviner light flash'd extacy o'er Heaven!
> Heav'n's hymnings paus'd: and Hell her yawning mouth
> Clos'd a brief moment.   (27–33)

4. The Process of his Doctrines on the mind of the Individual (33–51)

The section begins with the shocking statement 'Lovely was the Death
/ Of Him, whose Life was Love!' but the poet is not referring to
the brutal death of the crucified Christ, but his spiritual death in
the mystic union with God which is the fate of all elect beings. It is
these to whom the poem now turns, with a description of the spiritual
death of individuals who will achieve unity with God. This process
had been described empirically by David Hartley in *Observations
on Man*, and it is akin to the Neoplatonic purification of the soul
through the denial of self. The hierarchy of perceptions, from ideas
of sense to imagination, ambition, self-interest, sympathy, theophany
(visible presence of God to man), and the moral sense, were possible
to all men; but very few were thought to attain the highest knowledge.
Coleridge's 'spirit' is one of the few and is thus an 'elect' being. At
length all his misperceptions, such as the belief in the Trinitarian
God of traditional theology, will be purged and he will progress to
the highest moral truths: the trinity of faith, hope, and charity in
1 Corinthians 13. At length the spirit will achieve mystic union with
the Godhead: 'And when all things shall be subdued unto him, then
shall the Son also himself be subject unto him that put all things under
him, that God may be all in all.'[7] In 1797 Coleridge referred to
Hartley's commentary on St Paul's passage in *Observations on Man*:

> Since God is the source of all good, and consequently must at last appear
> to be so, *i.e..* be associated with all our pleasures, it seems to follow, even
> from this proposition, that the idea of God, and of the ways by which his
> goodness and happiness are made manifest, must, at last, take place of, and
> absorb all other ideas, and HE himself become, according to the language
> of the scriptures, *all in all* . . . (*Observations on Man*, i. 114)

[7] 1 Cor. 15: 28.

> Lovely was the Death
> Of Him, whose Life was Love! Holy with power
> He on the thought-benighted Sceptic beam'd
> Manifest Godhead, melting into day
> What Mists dim-floating of Idolatry
> Split and misshap'd the Omnipresent Sire:
> And first by TERROR, Mercy's startling prelude,
> Uncharm'd the Spirit spell-bound with earthly lusts
> Till of it's nobler Nature it 'gan feel
> Dim recollections; and thence soar'd to HOPE,
> From HOPE and stronger FAITH to perfect LOVE
> Attracted and absorb'd: and center'd there
> GOD only to behold, and know, and feel,
> Till by exclusive Consciousness of GOD
> All self-annihilated it shall make
> GOD it's Identity: God all in all!
> We and our Father ONE!   (33–51)

5. *Character of the Elect (51–135a)*

The 'elect beings' who are able to climb this ladder of perfectibility through the hierarchy of existence to come to a perfect vision of God are now identified as moral agents of the deity. With a perfect understanding of the inner order of the world, they are able to become immanent organic principles of divine action. In this longest section of the poem Coleridge develops his two principal themes: the perfectibility of individuals and the progression of all creation towards the millennial age. He begins with a restatement of the hierarchic scale of nature through the orders of creation:

> And gazing, trembling, patiently ascend
> Treading beneath their feet all visible things
> As steps, that upward to their Father's Throne
> Lead gradual—else nor glorified nor lov'd.
> THEY nor Contempt imbosom nor Revenge:
> For THEY dare know of what may seem deform
> The SUPREME FAIR sole Operant . . .   (56–62)

Rereading this passage two decades later, Coleridge shuddered at the suggestion of pantheism in the lines, and wrote in April 1814 to his old publisher Joseph Cottle:

The declaration that the Deity is 'the sole Operant' is indeed far too bold; may easily be misconstrued into Spinosism . . . I should by no means now use such a phrase. I was very young when I wrote that poem, and my religious feelings were more settled than my theological notions. (*CL* iii. 467)

Beginning his historical account of mankind's progressiveness, the poet introduces Old Testament imagery in the battling armies of the old religious wars when Yahweh the God of the Israelites rode in the tent of the Covenant:

> Their's too celestial courage, inly arm'd —
> Dwarfing Earth's giant brood, what time they muse
> On their great Father, great beyond compare!
> And marching onwards view high o'er their heads
> His waving Banners of Omnipotence.
>
> Who the Creator love, created might
> Dread not: within their tents no Terrors walk.   (65–71)

In a concise passage which echoes the traditional European ballad of 'the chase' the poet distinguishes between Old Testament times when man was less advanced and God was perceived with fear, and modern times when he is perceived with love. The Christian allegory of putting on the armour of God echoes Bunyan's Pilgrim. The modern age, however, is filled with millennial forebodings and seems 'terrible' as the angels of the Apocalypse prepare to empty their lethal vessels upon the earth. Yet the elect being understands that nature is merely being purged of an illness occasioned by man's abuses:

> GOD's Altar grasping with an eager hand
> FEAR, the wild-visag'd, pale, eye-starting wretch,
> Sure-refug'd hears his hot pursuing fiends
> Yell at vain distance. Soon refresh'd from Heaven
> He calms the throb and tempest of his heart.
> His countenance settles: a soft solemn bliss
> Swims in his eye: his swimming eye uprais'd:
> And Faith's whole armour glitters on his limbs!
> And thus transfigured with a dreadless awe,
> A solemn hush of soul, meek he beholds
> All things of terrible seeming. Yea, and there,
> Unshudder'd, unaghasted, he shall view
> E'en the SEVEN SPIRITS, who in the latter day
> Will shower hot pestilence on the sons of men.   (74–87)

Nature as sick or weary was a common reference in millennial writing, and in his notebook Coleridge jotted: 'Like a mighty

Giantess, / Seized in sore travail & prodigious birth / Sick Nature
struggled.'[8] He cures the illness with the parable of the Good
Samaritan and the 'good man', the healing Christ:

> And at the wells of renovating LOVE
> Fill their Seven Vials with salutary wrath,
> To sickly Nature more medicinal
> That what soft balm the weeping good man pours
> Into the lone despoiled trav'llers wounds!   (92–6)

Two years later when Coleridge revised the passage for the second
edition of 1797, he changed the tense of these lines to emphasize
the urgency of the last days of the world:

>   meek he beholds
> All things of terrible seeming: yea, unmov'd
> Views e'en th'immitigable ministers
> That shower down vengeance on these latter days.
> For kindling with intenser Deity
> From the celestial MERCY-SEAT they come,
> And at the renovating Wells of LOVE
> Have fill'd their Vials with salutary Wrath

>   (1797, 79–86)

Coleridge began the poem in the guise of a shepherd, using the
eighteenth-century convention which saw the shepherd most closely
bound to nature, for as the least spoilt member of society the
shepherd had retained the original 'state of nature'. Yet as the
associationist principles begin to operate on the experience of the
shepherd, he is transformed into a 'young angel'. In place of ideas
of self-interest, he is now able to perceive the beauty and oneness
of Creation:

> As when a Shepherd on a vernal morn
> Thro' some thick fog creeps tim'rous with slow foot,
> Darkling he fixes on th'immediate road
> His downward eye: all else of fairest kind
> Hid or deform'd. But lo, the bursting Sun!
>
>   . . . . . .
>
> He from his small particular orbit flies
> With blest outstarting! From HIMSELF he flies,
> Stands in the Sun, and with no partial gaze

                    [8] CN i. 199.

> Views all creation, and he loves it all,
> And blesses it, and calls it very good!   (103–7, 118–22)

The last line is taken from the Creation in Genesis: 'And God saw every thing that he had made, and, behold, it was very good.' In the journey of an elect being from the state of nature through the hierarchy of existence to the Godhead, the poet demonstrates that the final stage is to become an actual part of the creative being of the deity.

> This is indeed to dwell with the most High!
> Cherubs and rapture-trembling Seraphim
> Can press no nearer to th'Almighty's Throne.   (123–5)

Yet in spite of his elevation, the elect being at present can see only the chaos of the world caused by those who have not climbed to the heights of perception. The meaning of this passage is obscured by clumsy construction. Although men are not conscious of their collective unity with God, their destructive acts against others become self-destructive through unconscious bonds. Hence the poet sees both aggressors and victims as injured. The final image of the section is an Apocalyptic 'sea of blood' from Revelation 16: 3:

> But that we roam unconscious, or with hearts
> Unfeeling of our universal Sire,
> And that in his vast family no Cain
> Injures uninjur'd (in her best aim'd blow
> Victorious MURDER a blind Suicide)
> Haply for this some younger Angel now
> Looks down on Human Nature: and, behold!
> A sea of blood bestrew'd with wrecks, where mad
> Embattling INTERESTS on each other rush
> With unhelm'd Rage!   (126–35)

6. Superstition (135b–72)

His evolution from shepherd to young angel complete, the poet contemplates the mass of mankind, each of whom acts as a self-interested centre of activity, rather in the manner of the atheistic doctrines that Coleridge criticized for expounding an internal fragmented activity. The superstitious or atheistic beliefs of the masses are the doctrine of the Trinity ('secondary Gods'), atheism, and—a major theme of the poem, 'self-interest'. Self-interest is a stage in Hartley's associationist psychology, but it has become a permanent state of being for those who have failed to perceive higher truths because they are unable to associate their ideas:

> 'Tis the sublime of man,
> Our noontide Majesty, to know ourselves
> Parts and proportions of one wond'rous whole:
> This fraternizes man, this constitutes
> Our charities and bearings. But 'tis God
> Diffus'd thro' all, that doth make all one whole;
> This the worst superstition, him except,
> Aught to desire, SUPREME REALITY!   (135–42)

Coleridge is once more transferring the 'proofs of natural to moral Sciences'. He makes the most pantheistic statement of the poem: ''tis God / Diffus'd thro' all, that doth make all one whole'. This is clearly to be seen alongside the metaphysics of his contemporaneous poem 'The Eolian Harp':

> And what if All of animated Life
> Be but as Instruments diversly fram'd
> That tremble into thought, while thro' them breathes
> One infinite and intellectual Breeze?
>
> . . . . .
>
> Thus *God* would be the universal Soul,
> Mechaniz'd matter th'organic harps,
> And each one's Tunes be that, which each calls *I*. —
>
> ('Rugby MS', fols. 31–2)

We too are 'parts and proportions' of the whole, and this 'fraternizes' us. The great principle of the French Revolution 'fraternité' thus acknowledges in society what metaphysics has already revealed in nature. Thus the French republicans must be right: they have correctly transferred the knowledge of science to society.

In a clever deceit the poetry continues by seeming to describe superstitious practices among the natives in South America and Africa. But then, in a reference to the 'bales of living anguish' of the slave trade, the reader realizes that it is the European who is perpetrating the superstition on the slave, and the 'skull-pil'd Temple' is equally to apply to the English Church for supporting such barbarisms:

O Fiends of SUPERSTITION! not that oft
Your pitiless rites have floated with man's blood
The skull-pil'd Temple, not for this shall wrath
Thunder against you from the Holy One!
But (whether ye th'unclimbing Bigot mock
With secondary Gods, or if more pleas'd
Ye petrify th'imbrothell'd Atheist's heart,
The Atheist your worst slave) I o'er some plain
Peopled with Death, and to the silent Sun
Steaming with tyrant-murder'd multitudes;
Or where mid groans and shrieks loud-laughing TRADE
More hideous packs his bales of living anguish;
I will raise up a mourning, O ye Fiends!   (144–56)

Without a pause a new image is introduced. Newton's system of the world is evoked as a model for the moral sphere as well as the natural order. God, like the sun at the centre of Newton's 'system of the world', acts with a kind of 'moral gravity', which the poet earlier referred to as true freedom. Without morality as a cohesive force in societies, human beings will remain in a lonely savage state, whatever the appearance to the contrary. Coleridge is attacking Godwin's notion of the independent man, who has the veneer of civilization, but sensuous and vicious principles. The poet captures his objections in the phrase 'smooth Savage':

Hiding the present God, whose presence lost,
The moral world's cohesion, we become
An Anarchy of Spirits! Toy-bewitch'd,
Made blind by lusts, disherited of soul
No common center Man, no common sire
Knoweth! A sordid solitary thing,
Mid countless brethren with a lonely heart
Thro' courts and cities the smooth Savage roams
Feeling himself, his own low Self the whole . . .   (158–66)

7. Digression to the Present War (173–211)

The poet now 'digresses' to the European war which England entered against France after the execution of Louis XVI in February 1793. Although begun by Austria and Prussia, ostensibly for the purpose of restoring the French monarchy, the hostilities had become more complex as annexing and partitioning of weaker States occurred. The poet castigates the two warmongering leaders, Catherine the Great of Russia and Frederick William II of Prussia, and describes the state of the European countries in the first half of 1795. However, he styles the whole war as an Old Testament conflict urged on by priests and kings, with Yahweh, the vengeful God, riding among the warriors.

There is ample evidence that Coleridge felt strongly about the war. 'I will not press on your recollection the awful Truth,' he wrote in *Conciones ad Populum*, 'that in the course of this calamitous Contest more than a Million of men have perished.'[9] Later, *The Watchman* was to contain harrowing reports of suffering in the 1794–5 campaign. Coleridge reserved some of his strongest criticism for the English Church and bishops, who gave overwhelming support for the war in the pulpits and in the House of Lords. Fast-day sermons he called 'Prayers of Hate to the God of Love'.[10] Coleridge was also aware of the economic and social effect of the war on the country, particularly when the price of flour reached famine level in the cold summer of 1795:

> THEE to defend, meek Galilæan! THEE
> And thy mild laws of Love unutterable,
> Mistrust and Enmity have burst the bands
> Of social Peace; and list'ning Treachery lurks
> With *pious* fraud to snare a brother's life;
> And childless widows o'er the groaning land
> Wail numberless; and orphans weep for bread!
> THEE to defend, dear Saviour of Mankind!
> THEE, Lamb of God! THEE, blameless Prince of Peace!   (175–83)

'It is recorded in the shuddering hearts of Christians,' Coleridge recorded in *Conciones ad Populum*, 'that while Europe is reeking with Blood, and smoking with unextinguished Fires, in a contest of unexampled crimes and unexampled calamities, every Bishop but one voted for the continuance of the War.'[11] Like the Canaanite priests of the Old Testament who sacrificed their children to the god Moloch, the British priests too, by urging the war, have sent their sons to death:

> Not least in savagery of holy zeal,
> Apt for the yoke, the race degenerate,
> Whom Britain erst had blush'd to call her sons!
> THEE to defend the Moloch Priest prefers

---

[9] *Lectures 1795*, 59.   [10] Ibid. 65.   [11] Ibid. 66.

> The prayer of hate, and bellows to the herd
> That Deity, ACCOMPLICE Deity
> In the fierce jealousy of waken'd wrath
> Will go forth with our armies and our fleets
> To scatter the red ruin on their foes!   (196–204)

8. Origin and Uses of Government and Property (212–61)

The war section of the poem was not a total digression from the subject of the poem, for with these further allusions to Old Testament times Coleridge has prepared the reader to return to the origins of society. In this, the final section of the original poem, Coleridge attempts to tell the story of mankind as a history of the development of knowledge of the fundamental truths of science and society, now being revealed in his own age.

Returning to a pre-Christian age he seeks the genesis of those evils which were so manifest in his own age. Firstly Rousseau's state of nature is evoked, in which, without property (and thus competition), agrarian man remained ignorant:

> In the primeval age a dateless while
> The vacant Shepherd wander'd with his flock
> Pitching his tent where'er the green grass wav'd.   (212–14)

It is imagination which has caused the fall of man into competition and self-interest. 'Whence arise our Miseries? Whence arise our Vices?' Coleridge asked in *The Watchman*, 'From *imaginary* Wants.'[12]

> But soon Imagination conjur'd up
> An host of new desires: with busy aim,
> Each for himself, Earth's eager children toil'd.
> So PROPERTY began, twy-streaming fount,
> Whence Vice and Virtue flow, honey and gall.   (215–19)

In *A Discourse on Inequality* (1755) Rousseau had written:

The first man who, having enclosed a piece of land, thought of saying 'This is mine' and found people simple enough to believe him, was the true founder of civil society. How many crimes, wars, murders; how much misery and horror the human race would have been spared if someone had pulled up the stakes and filled in the ditch and cried out to his fellow men: 'Beware of listening to this imposter. You are lost if you forget that the fruits of the

[12] p. 130

earth belong to everyone and that the earth itself belongs to no one!' (opening
to part 2; trans. M. Crauston (Harmondsworth, 1984), 109)

In his notebook Coleridge noted the tradition that this first man was
Cain, who 'put an end to that simplicity in which men lived before
the invention of weights and measure'.[13] But the disciple of David
Hartley cannot believe that imagination and self-interest are wholly
bad. They are the initial stages and springs for mankind's spiritual
journey and they created civilization:

> Hence the soft couch, and many-colour'd robe,
> The timbrel, and arch'd dome and costly feast
> With all th'inventive arts, that nurs'd the soul
> To forms of beauty . . .   (220–3)

The passage is not concerned about the results of man's activity, for
the poet is not interested in relating the external history of nations.
His lines relate the development of perception and the cognitive
process itself:

> all th'inventive arts, that nurs'd the soul
> To forms of beauty, and by sensual wants
> Unsensualiz'd the mind, which in the means
> Learnt to forget the grossness of the end,
> Best pleasur'd with its own activity.   (222–6)

The poem's optimism now becomes apparent as Coleridge relates
how each evil is only the 'immediate source / Of mightier good':

>   Their keen necessities
> To ceaseless action goading human thought
> Have made earth's reasoning animal her Lord;
> And the pale-featur'd Sage's trembling hand
> Strong as an host of armed Deities!
> From Avarice thus, from Luxury and War
> Sprang heavenly Science: and from Science Freedom.   (232–8)

This is a good argument. Once it is realized that sensual delights
are perceived by the senses, and are not 'in' objects themselves (the
distinction made in Locke's primary and secondary qualities), people
begin to take delight in their mental processes. The exercise of these
faculties gave man knowledge and understanding, and so he became

[13] CN i. 277.

better able to mould his world: 'From Avarice thus, from Luxury and War / Sprang heavenly Science: and from Science Freedom.' That is the leitmotif of *Religious Musings*.

From this point the argument unfolds quickly. The elect band is recalled from the earlier sections of the poem. Only they, the philosophers and poets, have achieved this state of mental and spiritual awareness, and it is these who, spreading outwards by sympathy, will effect change in society. Coleridge knew that the popular radical movement of the 1790s had 'waken'd' the lower classes to the possibility of reform, but this was to be evolutionary not revolutionary: 'not to be procured by the tumultuous uprising of an indignant multitude but this final result of an unresisting yet deeply principled Minority, which gradually absorbing kindred minds shall at last become the whole'.[14]

> O'er waken'd realms Philosophers and Bards
> Spread in concentric circles: they whose souls
> Conscious of their high dignities from God
> Brook not Wealth's rivalry; and they who long
> Enamour'd with the charms of order hate
> Th'unseemly disproportion . . .   (239–44)

The elect band are to follow the example of Franklin, the paradigm philosopher of nature who became a great political leader and social engineer. Alluding to the 'phalanx' of Satan's army in book I of *Paradise Lost*, the poetry makes clear how strong mankind has become through the control of the heavens:

> that blest triumph, when the PATRIOT SAGE
> Call'd the red lightnings from th'o'er-rushing cloud
> And dash'd the beauteous Terrors on the earth
> Smiling majestic. Such a phalanx ne'er
> Measur'd firm paces to the calming sound
> Of Spartan flute!   (247–52)

Although the 'fated day' of revolution had yet to dawn, Coleridge puts it in the past tense, seeming to regard it as inevitable. 'Eloquent man', the political radicals such as John Thelwall, will rouse the masses, but these have not the knowledge of the world to bring about the new society. Hence, the elect must wait:

[14] *Lectures 1795*, 218.

> These on the fated day,
> When stung to rage by Pity eloquent men
> Have rous'd with pealing voice th'unnumber'd tribes
> That toil and groan and bleed, hungry and blind,
> These hush'd awhile with patient eye serene
> Shall watch the mad careering of the storm . . .   (252–7)

Chaos will again come to the world of men. Then, acting as agents of the creative power of God, the elect will 'tame' the storm to bring about the new millennial age that has only been dreamed of:

> Then o'er the wild and wavy chaos rush
> And tame th'outrageous mass, with plastic might
> Moulding Confusion to such perfect forms,
> As erst were wont, bright visions of the day!
> To float before them, when, the Summer noon,
> Beneath some arch'd romantic rock reclin'd
> They felt the sea-breeze lift their youthful locks,
> Or in the month of blossoms, at mild eve,
> Wandering with desultory feet inhal'd
> The wafted perfumes, and the flocks and woods,
> And many-tinted streams and setting Sun
> With all his gorgeous company of clouds
> Extatic gaz'd! then homeward as they stray'd
> Cast the sad eye to earth, and inly mus'd
> Why there was Misery in a world so fair.   (260–72)

Here in a confident and optimistic mood in the summer of 1795, Coleridge ended 'The Nativity' at 'not quite three hundred Lines'.[15]

But this is not, of course, the end of the poem that was published six months later as *Religious Musings*. What is most striking about 'The Nativity' is the extraordinary confidence and optimism of the lines. Coleridge began it in December 1794, the month that the treason trials of the leading reformers in England collapsed in a humiliating defeat for Pitt's government. But despite this there was no real ground for optimism. The leaders of the movement for reform of the parliamentary system did not expect to achieve any immediate concessions from the government. Although they had popular support from the lower classes, they had little political power, and the reformers were countered by an effective network of reactionary

---

[15] Letter to Cottle, Oct. 1795; *CL* i. 162.

'Church and King' associations which also claimed popular support, and could certainly mobilize the mob.

In France, though Robespierre was dead after two years of the Terror, the Revolution was still wading in the blood of many of her brightest citizens, and was certainly not a model of enlightened social change. Moreover, the social conditions in Britain, as wages dropped and food prices soared, were becoming very harsh.

Yet none of these facts could apparently shake Coleridge's confidence. 'The Nativity' set the progress of mankind firmly in the hands of radical intellectuals like William Godwin, John Thelwall, Erasmus Darwin, and Joseph Priestley, not one of them possessing substantial political power. The moral improvement in society was to be gradual and steady, and could not be disturbed by obdurate governments and revolutions. Society was to achieve a mild reparadised world, overseen by a 'small but glorious band . . . of thinking and disinterested Patriots'[16] sufficiently detached from the tempest of society to pursue their goals 'with patient eye serene'. Throughout 'The Nativity' there is confidence that natural phenomena will direct the minds of men towards higher truths, and Coleridge assumes that once such ideas have rooted in the mind, they will become moral truths by the necessity of association and so will be expressed in society.

In its original form 'The Nativity' is thus a didactic poem, with its emphasis throughout on education and teaching: the example of Christ, the scientific truths of the natural world, the moral truths of higher knowledge. The agents of this are the elect band of philosophers and bards; and, although he has some doubts, Coleridge expects that in changing English society his band will not meet the fate of their French counterparts:

Accustomed to regard all the affairs of man as a process, they never hurry and they never pause; theirs is not that twilight of political knowledge which gives us just light enough to place one foot before the other; as they advance, the scene still opens upon them, and they press right onward with a vast and various landscape of existence around them. (*Lectures 1795*, 12)

Coleridge wrote this in February 1795 and, what is more, believed it for most of the year. The collapse of the treason trials in December 1794 had released the radical patriots to work once more among

---

[16] *Lectures 1795*, 12.

the people, and they were winning large audiences at open-air rallies to protest at government policy. By late summer, having finished the revisions of *Joan of Arc*, Coleridge began to collect material for his first book of poems, which was to end with the completed 'Nativity'. By late October, marriage and move to Clevedon accomplished, Coleridge had finished the collection, and wrote to his publisher Joseph Cottle promising the remaining material any day.

On 26 October 1795 a mass meeting of the radical movement was held in London, addressed by, among others, William Frend and John Thelwall, who demanded an end to the French war and called for parliamentary reform. Three days later King George III was jostled by an angry crowd on his way to open parliament. On his return journey down the Mall two shots were fired at the king. The country was outraged and the radicals were blamed. At the beginning of November Pitt's government introduced two bills into parliament, banning meetings of over 50 people and making treasonable a variety of ill-defined activities such as writing or speaking with the intent to harm the king. Throughout the country loyalist meetings were held to give public thanks for the safety of the king's person and to draft letters condemning those behind the attack.

The citizens of Bristol met in the Guildhouse on 17 November to 'congratulate his Majesty on his late providential escape from the attack and insult offered to his person, and to show their utmost abhorrence of such proceedings'.[17] Thomas Beddoes was there, as was Coleridge, who, after listening to the loyalist declarations, bravely took the floor:

> He began by expressing his astonishment at the paradoxes he had heard: he said, that the whole business was a paradox. If the outrage on his Majesty's person was a great evil (and it certainly was) the best method to disapprove of it, and to prevent a repetition of such evils, was to remove the cause: the insult would never have been offered, if the people had not been rendered outrageous by their sufferings under the present cruel, sanguinary, and calamitous war. . . . 'Though the war,' said he, 'may take much from the property of the rich, it left them much: but a PENNY taken from the pocket of a poor man might deprive him of a dinner.'
> He was here authoritatively stopped . . . (*Lectures 1795*, 361)

---

[17] The *Star*'s report of the Bristol meeting appeared on 23 Nov. and is published in *Lectures 1795*, 359–62.

All thoughts of finishing his collection of poems were abandoned as Coleridge embarked on the month of pamphleteering and lecturing allowed before the bills became law and his activities treasonable. On 26 November he gave a lecture at Bristol on the two bills and early in December published this as *The Plot Discovered*. Towards the end of this address he used the final image in 'The Nativity' — of the control of electricity in the heavens — as a means of commenting on social control:

By the operation of Lord Grenville's Bill, the Press is made useless. Every town is insulated: the vast conductors are destroyed by the which the electric fluid of truth was conveyed from man to man, and nation to nation. (*Lectures 1794*, 313)

Thus the poetic solution to the problems in society of 'The Nativity' was now useless. The 'elect sages' who would have acted on the forces of inequality in society like moral lightning conductors were silenced and their quills banned. There could be no more progress in the moral order.

Coleridge's courage throughout the months which followed the attack on the king should not be discounted. He had known violence against reformers during his time at Cambridge, and delivered his political lectures earlier in the year despite threats.[18] But the fear of what might happen in England if the means of communicating truth was stopped outweighed personal fear: 'We will join the still small voice of reason, ere yet it be overwhelmed in the great and strong wind, in the earthquake, and in the fire!' he wrote in *The Plot Discovered*. It was this commitment that led Coleridge to create *The Watchman* to overcome the silence in the country after the bills became law at the beginning of December.

Not until February, after the launch of *The Watchman*, did Coleridge turn again to his collection of poetry. 'The Nativity' had dated considerably in the intervening five months and could no longer be considered finished. The calm, leisurely solution to the ills of mankind suddenly appeared wholly inadequate to the critical times in the country.

---

[18] 'Two or three uncouth and unbrained Automata have threatened my Life — and in the last Lecture the Genus infimum were scarcely restrained from attacking the house in which the "damn'd Jacobine was jawing away" ' (letter to Dyer, Feb. 1795; *CL* i. 152).

In February 1796 Coleridge began to add to 'The Nativity', writing a section which he titled 'The Present State of Society'. It began with an allegory of the event that had caused all the trouble and so changed the political climate of the country, the attack on George III four months earlier:

> O *blest* Society!
> Fitliest depictur'd by some sun-scorcht waste,
> Where oft majestic thro' the tainted noon
> The SIMOOM sails, before whose purple pomp
> Who falls not prostrate dies! And where, by night,
> Fast by each precious fountain on green herbs
> The lion crouches; or hyæna dips
> Deep in the lucid stream his bloody jaws;
> Or serpent rolls his vast moon-glittering bulk,
> Caught in whose monstrous twine Behemoth yells,
> His bones loud crashing!   (279–89)

Coleridge wrote in a draft revision of these lines that the image of the poisonous Simoom wind was 'emblematical of the pomp & power of Despotism'.[19] But the animals who crowd round to pollute the precious fountain of truth are also political allegories. 'Truth is compared in scripture to a streaming fountain; if her waters flow not in perpetual progression, they stagnate into a muddy pool of conformity & tradition. Milton', Coleridge noted.[20] In *The Plot Discovered* he had described the Prime Minister William Pitt as the 'old Serpent', conceiving and laying bills 'in the dunghill of despotism'.[21]

'The Present State of Society' reviewed the present condition of the poorest members of society, the criminals and prostitutes, parish-widows and the sick, soldiers and war-widows. Yet here Coleridge's own prejudices begin to show, for he portrayed these classes as so brutalized by their experiences that they had themselves become brutes:

> O ye numberless,
> Whom foul Oppression's ruffian gluttony
> Drives from life's plenteous feast! O thou poor Wretch,
> Who nurs'd in darkness and made wild by want
> Dost roam for prey, yea thy unnatural hand
> Liftest to deeds of blood!   (289–94)

---

[19] Deleted revision for the second edition in 1797; BL MS Ashley 408, fol. 33.
[20] CN i. 119.   [21] *Lectures 1795*, 288.

This is the spectacle of the mob, whom the poet has already referred to as the 'herd', as a 'wild and wavy chaos', 'outrageous mass', and, in *Joan of Arc*, an 'infected Throng'.[22] It was Coleridge's enduring prejudice throughout his radical youth that without middle-class reformers to educate and guide the people to reform, rebellion by violent and uncontrollable masses was inevitable: 'The Patriots of France', he wrote in *A Moral and Political Lecture*, 'were sacrificed by the Mob, with whose prejudices and ferocity their unbending Virtue forbade them to assimilate. Like Sampson, the People were strong—like Sampson, the People were blind.'[23] He has described the poor, but without the power of the elect band, lacks the means to transform them. So they are advised to:

> Rest awhile,
> Children of Wretchness! More groans must rise,
> More blood must st[r]eam, or ere your wrongs be full.   (313–15)

With no practical solution to the problem of how successful change is to be effected when those who should control it are silenced by law, Coleridge retreats into biblical dogma. Continue to suffer, he exhorts the people, because the end of the world is nearly upon us. Do not worry; for the cup of wrongs is almost full and if you suffer more it will overflow to waken those other Children of Wretchedness, the martyrs:

> Yet is the day of Retribution nigh:
> The Lamb of God hath open'd the fifth seal:
> And upward rush on swiftest wing of fire
> Th'innumerable multitude of Wrongs
> By man on man inflicted! Rest awhile,
> Children of Wretchness! The hour is nigh:
> And lo! the Great, the Rich, the Mighty Men,
> The Kings and the Chief Captains of the World,
> With all that fix'd on high like stars of Heaven
> Shot baleful influence, shall be cast to earth,
> Vile and down-trodden, as the untimely fruit
> Shook from the fig-tree by a sudden storm.   (316–27)

Coleridge now settles for the conventional apocalyptic vision of the French Revolution, a purifying storm that has purged the

---

[22] *Religious Musings*, 200, 258, 259; *Joan of Arc*, ii. 449.
[23] *Lectures 1795*, 6.

Whore of Mystery, and will soon reveal a pantisocratic paradise on earth:

> for lo! the Giant FRENZY
> Uprooting empires with his whirlwind arm
> Mocketh high Heaven . . .   (330–2)
>   She hath fallen
> On whose black front was written MYSTERY;
> She that reel'd heavily, whose wine was blood;
> She that work'd whoredom with the DÆMON POWER
> And from the dark embrace all evil things
> Brought forth and nurtur'd . . .   (342–7)

> Return pure FAITH! return meek PIETY!
> The kingdoms of the world are your's: each heart
> Self-govern'd, the vast family of Love
> Rais'd from the common earth by common toil
> Enjoy the equal produce.   (352–6)

At the opening of the poem Christ was described as the 'Good Man'. Now the poet takes on this role: one of the visionary band who are allowed a glimpse of the paradisaical world that will be the new age:

> Such delights
> As float to earth, permitted visitants!
>   .   .   .   .   .   .
> The favor'd good man in his lonely walk
> Perceives them, and his silent spirit drinks
> Strange bliss which he shall recognize in heaven.
> And such delights, such strange beatitude
> Seize on my young anticipating heart
> When that blest future rushes on my view!
>
>   (356–7, 365–70)

This new section of the poem was published in the second issue of *The Watchman* on 9 March 1796. Readers were told that it was an extract from *Religious Musings*, the first mention of the new title for the year-old poem. Coleridge thought that the section had completed the poem, and he wrote to Cottle: 'The Religious Musings are finished, and you shall have them on Thursday.'[24] But it was not possible to print the new version: the collection of poems now

---

[24] Letter of early Mar. 1796; CL 187.

required an extra sheet to print it, only a quarter of which would be used by the poem.

After 15 months Coleridge thus began to write the final sections of *Religious Musings*, filling the remaining space in the volume. Cottle still remembered this 40 years later: 'A part of the poem was even written after all before in the volume was printed; the press being suspended till he had progressively completed it.'[25] Coleridge's manuscript bears this out: 'Room for [six, eight lines *del.*] sixteen lines', he noted towards the end. It was not the last time he would write to fill space in a publication. The state of the text of *Religious Musings* in the first edition shows that it was set without much care.[26] Three lines (18–20) were omitted from the text without direction in the manuscript, and the numbering of lines is thus wrong throughout. The manuscript reads:

> Yet Thou, than all th'Angelic Blaze, more bright,
> Despised *Galilaean*! Man of Woes!
> When poor and mean and hungry thou didst roam
> Placeless to hide thy all unshelter'd Head,
> Where slept the nested Bird and cavern'd Brute.
> For chiefly in th'oppressed Good Man's Face . . .
>
> ('Rugby MS', 16–21)

The last three sheets to be printed, signature M, N, A, are much poorer impressions than the rest of the volume, and during the printing of sheet M the printer ran out of paper and had to use old stock. Moreover, the notes to *Religious Musings* were clearly printed before the last sections of the poetry were written, so the single note from this part ('DAVID HARTLEY') appears as a footnote beneath the text. On 28 March, however, Cottle wrote Coleridge a receipt for the poems[27] and *Poems on Various Subjects* was finally published on 16 April 1796.

Despite all the constraints, the latter part of *Religious Musings* contains some of its most successful poetry, and Coleridge does achieve a synthesis of the diverse strands of his complex work. The

[25] Joseph Cottle, *Early Recollections; chiefly relating to the late Samuel Taylor Coleridge, during his long residence in Bristol*, 2 vols. (1837), ii. 52.
[26] These bibliographical details were first noted by F. C. Stephens, 'Cottle, Wise and *MS Ashley 408*', *Bibliographical Society of America Papers*, lxviii (1974), 396.
[27] E. L. Griggs printed the receipt in *CL* i. 195.

final sections of the poem are 'Millenium, Universal Redemption, Conclusion'.

Confident about the imminent approach of the final stage of the world, the poet reinterprets the millennial reign of the martyrs in Revelation 20: 4 as the rule of the philosophers of the ancient knowledge who have preserved the truths of natural and revealed religion for the modern age. Drafts of the passage give Plato and Socrates, but the published version mentions only four: Milton, Newton, Hartley, and Priestley. Undoubtedly chosen because they are the most important influences in *Religious Musings*, they thus continue the self-referential nature of the poetry. Indeed, a significant self-reference after the triple accolade to Priestley ('Patriot, and Saint, and Sage') shows exactly what unites the *prisca theologia* and the intellectual tradition of the eighteenth century. It is the poet; for Coleridge himself is the next stage in the ancient tradition:

> The mighty Dead
> Rise to new life, whoe'er from earliest time
> With conscious zeal had urg'd Love's wond'rous plan
> Coadjutors of God.   (376–9)

> There to PLATO's gaze
> Sweep brighter Visions than on elder days

> ('Rugby MS', fol. 56)

> He of ancient days
> Wisest, nor haply uninspir'd of God
> Mild Socrates

> ('Rugby MS', fol. 58)

> To MILTON's trump
> The odorous groves of earth reparadis'd
> Unbosom their glad echoes: inly hush'd
> Adoring NEWTON his serener eye
> Raises to heaven: and he of mortal kind
> Wisest, he* first who mark'd the ideal tribes
> Down the fine fibres from the sentient brain
> Roll subtly-surging. Pressing on his steps
> Lo! Priestley there, Patriot, and Saint, and Sage,
> Whom that my fleshly eye hath never seen . . .   (379–88)

> *DAVID HARTLEY.

Coleridge now shows how comfortably he could move between ancient and modern traditions. After reading *The True Intellectual*

System he noted: 'The father of all gods the ocean is, Tethys their mother.'[28] Cudworth had interpreted this passage from Plato as a description of the waters of chaos, and this agrees with Coleridge's reference to 'Old OCEAN' in *Religious Musings*:

> The THOUSAND YEARS lead up their mystic dance,
> Old OCEAN claps his hands! the DESERT shouts!
> And soft gales wafted from the haunts of Spring
> Melt the primaeval North!   (373–6)

The desert is a common millennial image, and is drawn from Isaiah 35: 1: 'The wilderness and the solitary place shall be glad for them; and the desert shall rejoice.' The two ancient images of the waters of chaos and the millennial desert thus symbolize the beginning and end of the 6,000-year span of the world. But the further millennial occurrence, the melting of polar ice-caps to control the winds and so bring about a perfect climate, is a contemporary idea described by Erasmus Darwin:

> Oh, SYLPHS! disclose in this inquiring age
> One GOLDEN SECRET to some favor'd sage;
> Grant the charm'd talisman, the chain, that binds,
> Or guides the changeful pinions of the winds!
>   . . . . . .
> Autumn and Spring in lively union blend,
> And from the skies the Golden Age descend.
>
> ('The Economy of Vegetation', iv. 307–10, 319–20)

Religious Musings is self-consciously a poem of apprenticeship. It had opened with the poet as a shepherd on the first Christmas morning, and translated him to an angel in the early part of the work. But in the second edition of 1797, Coleridge rewrote the opening, and recast himself as an angel from the beginning, evidently believing that the heady years of 1795 and 1796 had taken him beyond 'young noviciate thought'[29]

> This is the time, when, most divine to hear,
> The voice of Adoration rouses me,
> As with Cherub's trump: and high upborne,
> Yea, mingling with the Choir, I seem to view

[28] CN i. 247.   [29] l. 429.

> The vision of the heavenly multitude,
> Who hymn'd the song of Peace o'er Bethlehem's fields!
>
> (*1797*, 1–6)

A similar change between the two editions occurs towards the end of the poem at the advent of the millennium. In the original version it is the author of Revelation who attends the age:

> O Years! the blest preeminence of Saints!
> Sweeping before the rapt prophetic Gaze
> Bright as what glories of the jasper throne
> Stream from the gorgeous and face-veiling plumes
> Of Spirits adoring!   (395–9)

But in *1797* it is the author of *Religious Musings* who sta_ds at the gateway to the millennium:

> O Years! the blest preeminence of Saints!
> Ye sweep athwart my gaze, so heavenly-bright,
> The wings that veil the adoring Seraph's eyes,
> What time he bends before the Jasper Throne
> Reflect no lovelier hues!
>
> (*1797*, 383–7)

A draft for the first edition emphasizes the apprenticeship:

> Aye, *blest* Years! must end
> But my soul tires, and my stretch'd Intellect
> Akes, as with growing pains: and Fancy now
> [Uprearing thro' the infinite of Truth *del.*]
> From these unmeasur'd and stupendous heights
> Fast-fluttering her vain pinions falls to earth
> And there lies panting . . .
>
> ('Rugby MS', fols. 57–8)

This interesting passage reveals the beginnings of Coleridge's struggle to understand his own imaginative faculty. 'Fancy' is rising through Truth, in a Platonic ascent through the levels of being. Yet it is also fluttering unsupported from a flight which might have merely been fanciful. In the published poem the poet remained pessimistic:

> Ye, blest Years! must end,
> And all beyond is darkness! Heights most strange!
> Whence Fancy falls, fluttering her idle wing.   (399–401)

In *Joan of Arc* Coleridge presented the creative spirit of God with a similar image: 'When LOVE rose glittering, and his gorgeous wings / Over the abyss flutter'd with such glad noise',[30] The association of 'fancy fluttering' at the beginning of the world recalls the reference to imagination in the primeval state in *Religious Musings*:

> In the primeval age a dateless while
> The vacant Shepherd wander'd with his flock
> Pitching his tent where'er the green grass wav'd.
> But soon Imagination conjur'd up
> An host of new desires . . .   (212–16)

The imagination thus appears in the poem as the human faculty which is responsible for the fall of man from innocence and ignorance, which yet urges man to higher and higher states of being, until at the end of time in the highest realm of existence, it falls vainly from the presence of God.

The poet now opts for a conventional retelling of Revelation, with the Devil roused for the final battle and the seventh angel of the apocalypse calling time:

> For who of woman born may paint the hour,
> When seiz'd in his mid course the Sun shall wane
> Making noon ghastly! Who of woman born
> May image in his wildly-working thought,
> How the black-visag'd, red-eyed Fiend outstretcht
> Beneath th'unsteady feet of Nature groans
> In feverish slumbers—destin'd then to wake,
> When fiery whirlwinds thunder his dread name
> And Angels shout, DESTRUCTION! How his arm
> The mighty Spirit lifting high in air
> Shall swear by Him, the ever-living ONE,
> TIME IS NO MORE!   (402–13)

He relates the mystical Neoplatonic moment when the world will be purged by fire; as the soul purified by divine fire is united with its divine source. This is the moment when Plato's Cave-men are released from their shackles and turn into the dazzling brightness of day:

---

[30] ii. 228–9.

> Believe thou, O my soul,
> Life is a vision shadowy of Truth,
> And vice, and anguish, and the wormy grave,
> Shapes of a dream! The veiling clouds retire,
> And lo! the Throne of the redeeming God
> Forth flashing unimaginable day
> Wraps in one blaze earth, heaven, and deepest hell.   (413-19)

In *1797* Coleridge wrote: 'This paragraph is intelligible to those, who, like the Author, believe and feel the sublime system of Berkley; and the doctrine of the final Happiness of all men.' A draft casts slightly more light on the paragraph:

> Like a Dream,
> Corporeal things shall vanish—and the Clouds
> Sudden retiring, from the throne of God
> Shall flash one blaze of all-restoring Light
> Involving Earth, & Heaven, & deepest Hell!
>
> ('Rugby MS', fol. 58)

George Berkeley had married his early idealistic philosophy to Platonism when he wrote *Siris* and portrayed the sensory world as a pointer to the real world of divine truth. What is corporeal is merely the veil of perception which hides reality. Coleridge wrote in his notebook:

In the paradisiacal World Sleep was voluntary & holy—a spiritual before God, in which the mind elevated by contemplation retired into pure intellect suspending all commerce with sensible objects & perceiving the present deity— (*CN* i. 191)

He saw this state as 'the doctrine of the final Happiness of all men', and thought that it would become a reality when all were able to read nature as the language of God, and see beyond the puzzling veil to God's immediate presence.

In the final section of *Religious Musings* Coleridge wrote perhaps the only lines of the poem that hint what he was to achieve, for his 'Conclusion' is a fine summary of the main themes of the poem. The two worlds of nature and of man are now brought together through the unity of divine principles of action in each, the plastic powers of nature and the band of elect beings of society. Rising to the marvellous 'And what if' of pure speculative thought, Coleridge now identifies these two worlds as part of the being and reality of God,

and pledges himself to them. The lines descend to a gentle image
of harmony between the divinity and his world, and so the poem
ends its desultory religious musings:

> Contemplant Spirits! ye that hover o'er
> With untir'd gaze th'immeasurable fount
> Ebullient with creative Deity!
> And ye of plastic power, that interfus'd
> Roll thro' the grosser and material mass
> In organizing surge! Holies of God!
> (And what if Monads of the infinite mind?)
> I haply journeying my immortal course
> Shall sometime join your mystic choir! Till then
> I discipline my young noviciate thought
> In ministries of heart-stirring song,
> And aye on Meditation's heaven-ward wing
> Soaring aloft I breathe th'empyreal air
> Of LOVE, omnific, omnipresent LOVE,
> Whose day-spring rises glorious in my soul
> As the great Sun, when he his influence
> Sheds on the frost-bound waters — The glad stream
> Flows to the ray and warbles as it flows.   (420–37)

7

The Vital Question

The force that through the green fuse drives the flower
Drives my green age; that blasts the roots of trees
Is my destroyer.

    Dylan Thomas, 'The force that through the green fuse'

AFTER the months of hiatus in which he had published *Poems on Various Subjects* and *The Watchman*, Coleridge had some time to plan ahead. Encouraged by the reception of his poetry, he reconsidered the plan for a second volume of longer poems, to include lines from Southey's *Joan of Arc* and a project called 'Hymns to the Sun, the Moon, and the Elements'.[1] Charles Lamb, his staunchest supporter at the time, mentioned these 'embryonic "hymns"' in a letter to Coleridge of 13 June 1796:

When they are mature of birth (were I you) I should print 'em in one separate volume, with 'Religious Musings' and your part of the 'Joan of Arc.' Birds of the same soaring wing should hold on their flight in company. (*Letters*, ed. Marrs, i. 28)

Coleridge's model for these Hymns was undoubtedly Erasmus Darwin's 'The Economy of Vegetation', which is also divided into four cantos on the ancient elements of Fire, Earth, Water, and Air. It seems strange, though, that Coleridge should even contemplate such a remote and philosophical project when only weeks before he had been caught up in radical politics and fears of violent revolution in Britain. Yet Coleridge was losing heart in the reforming cause. The repressive measures which Pitt's government had introduced at the end of 1795 did effectively stifle the radicals, and despite Coleridge's warnings of social catastrophes, the leaders of the reforming movement were silenced without either side resorting to violence. Those radical philosophers to whom Coleridge had looked for a lead in the anticipated moral storm resumed their original scientific activities and much of the impetus of the radical movement was halted.

---

[1] One of Coleridge's numerous lists of projected works; *CN* i. 174 [16]

Thomas Beddoes now became more important to Coleridge. The two men had campaigned together in the winter of 1795–6 for the repeal of the Gagging Bills, but in 1796 Beddoes became fully involved with the Pneumatic Institution at Clifton, where his patients and friends were used as guinea-pigs to investigate the therapeutic powers of newly discovered gases like nitrous oxide and carbon monoxide. Beddoes was also checking the proofs of Darwin's second volume of *Zoonomia*, and arguing with its author, an old friend, about the principle of vitality.[2] In May 1796, perhaps inspired by talking with Beddoes, Coleridge wrote to Thomas Poole about a plan to visit Jena University and to teach on his return to England 'Man as Animal: including the complete knowledge of Anatomy, Chemistry, Mechanics & Optics'.[3] For Jena was where Johann Blumenbach taught, one of the leading authorities of the day on theories of life and generation.

Although the advances made in chemistry by Priestley and Lavoisier suggested that many living processes could be described in material terms, most philosophers still asserted the need for a vital principle beyond the limits of natural science. As life was something possessed by only a small part of the natural world, and by this for only a short time, it was generally thought that the principle of vitality was something given to organic bodies at their conception and taken from them at death. Thus while significant advances had been made in man's understanding of other active processes in the world, such as combustion, electricity, magnetism, and chemical affinity, it was thought that the principle of life should be different from these *in kind*, for if not, the barrier between the living and non-living world would disappear, obscuring the need for a giver of life. In the eighteenth century there were three schools of thought about vitality: the first denied that it was anything added to living things, the second believed the 'added' principle was a fine material substance, and the third held it to be a spiritual substance.

By the end of 1796, conversations and research for his 'Hymns' had made Coleridge confident enough to try out his own ideas on life with an established expert on the subject, John Thelwall, whose

---

[2] This correspondence is in John Stock, *Memoirs of the Life of Thomas Beddoes, M.D. with an analytical account of his writings* (London, 1811), App. 6, pp. xxxv–xlvii.

[3] Letter of May 1796; *CL* i. 209.

thoughts on vitality were published in *An Essay towards a definition of Animal Vitality: read at the Theatre, Guy's Hospital, January 26, 1793; in which several of the opinions of the Celebrated John Hunter are examined and controverted*.[4] On 31 December 1796 Coleridge wrote to Thelwall:

— Dr Beddoes, & Dr Darwin think that *Life* is utterly inexplicable, writing as Materialists — You, I understand, have adopted the idea that it is the result of organized matter acted on by external Stimuli. — As likely as any other system; but you *assume* the thing to be proved — the *'capability'* of being stimulated into sensation' *as a property* of organized matter — now 'the Capab.' &c is *my* definition of *animal Life* — Monro believes in a plastic immaterial Nature — all-pervading —

> And what if all of animated Nature
> Be but organic harps diversely fram'd
> That tremble into *thought* as o'er them sweeps
> Plastic & vast &c —

. . . Hunter that the *Blood* is the Life — which is saying nothing at all — for if the blood were *Life*, it could never be otherwise than Life — and to say, it is *alive*, is saying nothing — & Ferriar believes in a *Soul*, like an orthodox Churchman — So much for Physicians & Surgeons — Now as to the Metaphysicians, Plato says, it is *Harmony* — He might as well have said, a fiddle stick's end — but I love Plato — his dear *gorgeous* Nonsense! And *I, tho' last not least, I* do not know what to think about it — on the whole, I have rather made up my mind that I am a mere *apparition* — a naked Spirit! — And that Life is I myself I! which is a mighty clear account of it. (*CL* i. 294–5)

Coleridge's ideas are in part taken from a paper by the physician and political radical John Ferriar.[5] Ferriar called the vital principle a 'living power independent of the mind',[6] and traced its pedigree from Plato's idea of plastic nature which mediated between body and

---

[4] A photocopy of this rare pamphlet is kept in the Radcliffe Science Library at Oxford.

[5] 'Observations concerning the Vital Principle', *Memoirs of the Lit. & Phil.* iii (1790), 216–41. The same volume contains the description of a 'glory' by John Haygarth which Coleridge noted in *CN* i. 258, and Ferriar, 'Of Popular Illusions, and particularly of Medical Demonology', traced by Lowes as a source of ocular imagery and animal magnetism in *The Ancient Mariner* (see Lowes, *Road to Xanadu*, 500, 518). Beer (*Coleridge's Poetic Intelligence*, 106) and R. Young ('The Life Within: *The Prelude* and Organic Form', unpublished D.Phil. thesis (Oxford, 1980), 192–201) discuss the sources of this letter.

[6] 'Observations concerning the Vital Principle', 238.

soul down to the seventeenth century, when the principle became confused with the plastic power of nature as a whole in the writings of the Neoplatonists More and Cudworth. He then described the three popular theories of the eighteenth century:

> Some philosophers began at length to imagine that matter might acquire vitality, in consequence of a certain organization. But while no single hypothesis respecting the vital principle prevailed generally, two theories appeared, which engaged attention by the eminence of their authors, as well as by their own nature. Dr. Munro accounts for the commencement of the involuntary motions, and some other phaenomena, on the supposition of a living principle, pervading the universe; similar, I apprehend, to the plastic nature of the Platonists. Mr. Hunter attributes to the blood, a power of forming and renewing parts, by its proper efforts, apparently carried, in some cases, almost to a degree of rationality. (pp. 221–2)

That life could arise from what Ferriar called 'a certain organization' of matter was the materialist theory of Joseph Priestley, who had attempted to remove the need for spiritual principles by redefining matter as point-sources of attraction and repulsion in *Disquisitions Relating to Matter and Spirit* (1777). This treatise, significant in the development of the physics of matter and force, is a disappointing contribution to the debate about the vital principle, for Priestley was unclear about the relationship between living and non-living matter and considered it sufficient to have proved that living processes, such as perception, could have arisen from his conception of matter: '*Different* as are the properties of sensation and thought, from such as are usually ascribed to matter,' he wrote, 'they may, nevertheless, inhere in the same substance, unless we can show them to be absolutely *incompatible* with one another.'[7] The problem with this materialism, as Thelwall pointed out in his *Essay*, was that it admits organized bodies which can 'lay no claim to any sort of Vitality'.[8] Moreover, as Ferriar noted in a later paper to Priestley's son-in-law, 'An Argument against the Doctrine of Materialism, addressed to Thomas Cooper, Esq.', while the followers of Priestley believed that the structure and organization of the brain alone was necessary to produce thought, 'the contrary seems to be probable from these facts, which shew that, at different times, every part of that structure has been deeply injured, or totally destroyed, without impeding or

---

[7] *Works*, iii. 281.   [8] *Essay towards a definition of Animal Vitality*, 32.

changing any part of the process of thought.'[9] Suddenly, from holding an unassailable position in Coleridge's thought, Priestley is absent from his letter and is attacked indirectly through Plato, whose idea of 'harmony' seemed to Coleridge to resemble Priestley's 'organization'.

This change in attitude is interesting. Coleridge's famous declaration to Robert Southey of two years earlier that he 'went further than Hartley' and believed in 'the corporeality of *thought*—namely that it is motion'[10] is plainly a materialist interpretation of Hartley's theory of associations. Coleridge could have read it in 1794 in the first volume of Darwin's *Zoonomia*, where it is asserted that ideas are received in the brain as physical miniatures of their objects and thus are nothing but 'motions' in nerve fibres. Beddoes was criticizing Darwin's views in 1796, using Berkeley's idealist philosophy as support, and it is thus quite extraordinary for Coleridge to inform Thelwall that Dr Darwin and Dr Beddoes were materialists, when Beddoes was an avowed idealist.[11] Yet, as has already been noted, there are precedents in Coleridge's attitude to Newton, Godwin, and Paine, where the poet used their fundamental ideas—Newton's aether, Godwin's elect band, Paine's nature as divine language— and then accused them of holding contrary views.

The 'vitalists' opposed those in the eighteenth century who attempted to produce a material account of the living principle, and held instead that there was a more fundamental distinction between living systems and dead or inert matter than mere material organization, and that a different principle or power was required to account for the phenomenon of organic life. Their chief supporter was the late John Hunter, the king's surgeon and one of the greatest physiologists of the century, whose researches had shown that the difference between living and dead matter lay in its chemical behaviour. Hunter had observed in a paper to the Royal Society titled 'On the Digestion of the Stomach after Death'[12] that while living creatures do not digest their own stomachs but only dead organic matter introduced

---

[9] *Memoirs of the Lit. & Phil.* iv. (1793), 22.

[10] Letter to Southey of 11 Dec. 1794; *CL* i. 137.

[11] 'After much attention to your reasoning, I cannot perceive any probability in the opinion that ideas resemble external objects; and I do not think this ingenious hypothesis will protect the material world against Berkeley's Essays and Dialogues' (Beddoes's letter to Darwin in Stock, *Memoirs of Beddoes*, p. xl).

[12] *Phil. Trans.* lxii (1772), 447–54.

into the stomach, after death autodigestion in the animal begins. This indicated, he argued, that some force or power, superior to chemical forces, protected and maintained living matter from the material processes of digestion. Only on the death of the individual, after the vital principle had ceased, was the body subject to ordinary chemical laws. In his *Treatise on the Blood, Inflammation, and Gun-Shot Wounds* (1794), published rather ironically after his death, Hunter located the vital principle in the blood, and argued that 'we grow out of it, and if it has not life previous to this operation, it must then acquire it in the act of forming.'[13] Thelwall's paper to Guy's Hospital was a critical appraisal of Hunter, who Thelwall correctly believed was influenced by the Judaic belief that the life of an animal was in its blood.[14] But he found Hunter's account rather less clear than that in Leviticus:

> The definition of John Hunter appears to be particularly vague and unsatisfactory. '*Life*,' he says, '*does not consist in any modification of matter*: it either is *something superadded to matter*, or else it consists in a *peculiar arrangement of certain fine particles of matter*, which, being *thus disposed*, acquire the properties of Life.' (*Essay towards a definition of Animal Vitality*, 34)

Reasonably dismissing the second definition as a mere restatement of the 'organization' theory which Hunter had wished to refute, Thelwall turned his attention to 'something superadded to matter', which he assumed was an immaterial and spiritual principle:

> if there is any such *thing* entering into the animal composition (though our senses have never yet been capable of taking cognizance of it) as *Spirit*, having an existence separate and distinct from organization, and that gross perishable kind of substance we call body . . . such *Spirit*, however subtle, however refined, must still be material: and then, indeed, the absurdity vanishes—because that more subtle matter can act upon that which is more gross and inert, we have sufficient evidence in the action of air, and of the electric fluid. (ibid.)

Invoking the tradition of 'imponderable fluids' between matter and spirit, Thelwall translated Hunter's theory to Neoplatonic plastic powers, and so gave it an affinity with the theory of the other

---

[13] *Treatise on the Blood*, p. 78.
[14] 'For the life of all flesh is the blood thereof' (Lev. 17: 14).

physician in Coleridge's letter, the Scot Dr Alexander Monro, *secundus*.

In his *Observations on the Structure and Functions of the Nervous System* of 1783 Monro had described the vital principle as 'the Power which created all things, which gave life to animals and motion to the heavenly bodies . . . [which] continues to act upon, and to maintain all, by the unceasing influence of a living principle pervading the universe, the nature of which our faculties are incapable of duly comprehending'.[15] Coleridge seemed pleased with this idea, for it gave this power a strong affinity with the 'intellectual Breeze' of his poem 'The Eolian Harp'. But Ferriar had criticized Monro's idea with an argument which should have been familiar to Coleridge. The 'plastic power' was either material or immaterial: if material, matter had inherent activity, and life might be explained without evoking imponderable matter; if immaterial, it was not obvious how it could control the physiological functions of organic bodies. Hence it was either redundant or ineffective. The argument is essentially that of Coleridge in his *Joan of Arc* criticism of Newton's aether. Indeed, Coleridge appears to recognize this, for in his manuscript notes 'Remarks &c on Atheism', probably written some weeks earlier, he numbered among those who make 'consciousness & reasoning' result from the essential qualities of '*atoms* of matter . . . almost all Surgeons, Chemists, & Scotch Physicians'.[16]

Behind the conspiratorial humour in this important letter to Thelwall is a confident and rather superior assessment of the theories. Thelwall believed that electricity was the active principle in living things, and was told by the young man that his theory was 'As likely as any other system', but warned not to take 'the "*capability* of being stimulated into sensation" as a *property* of organised matter'. Once more Coleridge is carping at empiricism, which pulls all principles of action in the universe into the mundane world that is perceived by the senses. By forcing the vital spirit to become what it plainly was not (i.e. wholly material), the demands of the empiricists could be met; but to penetrate the mysteries of life it was necessary to go further. It is perhaps for this reason that Coleridge placed his own thought among the 'Metaphysicians'.

Yet there is also a suggestion of the elect tradition in Coleridge's mind. Truly elect individuals have no reason to adhere to the

[15] p. 104.　　　[16] BL MS Egerton 2801, fol. 215; also in *Lectures 1795*, 101 n.

mundane principles of empiricism. Once they have ascended to the higher levels of perception their finer senses can pierce through the 'veil' of the material world to the causal world beyond. Thus they escape the demands of the mundane philosophy of the physical world.

The concluding remarks of Isaac Newton in *Principia* about 'a certain most subtle spirit which pervades and lies hid in all gross bodies'[17] was the stimulus for a century of research into the active forces of gravitation, electricity, magnetism, and light in nature. Relating the state of knowledge of these forces in 'The Economy of Vegetation' Erasmus Darwin explained that heat, electricity, and magnetism were supposed to be fluids of different gravities, 'heat being the heaviest of them, electricity the next heavy, and magnetism the lightest'.[18] He suggested that the vital principle was another particular fluid:

there would seem to be another material received from the air by respiration; which is so necessary to life, that the embryon must learn to breath[e] almost within a minute after its birth, or it dies. The perpetual necessity of breathing shews, that the material thus acquired is perpetually consuming or escaping, and on that account requires perpetual renovation. Perhaps the spirit of animation itself is thus acquired from the atmosphere, which if it be supposed to be finer or more subtle than the electric matter, could not long be retained in our bodies, and must therefore require perpetual renovation. (i. 401 n.)

Although Darwin believed that the spirit of animation was different from other fluids, the similarity of the effects of the vital principle and the animating forces in nature inevitably led to closer comparisons. By the end of the eighteenth century the influence of gravitational, magnetic, electrical, and luminous fluids on living things had been described, and several important attempts were made to identify the vital principle with one or other of these imponderable fluids.

In his classification of disease *Zoonomia* Darwin updated the ancient tradition which described the influence of phases of the sun and moon on the health of creatures. He listed 11 types of diseases which show periodic variations due to heavenly bodies, including hydrophobia, piles, and gout, and discussed also the influence of lunar cycles on menstruation.[19] These influences could not be

---

[17] General Scholium to bk. III; trans. Andrew Motte (1729), 547.
[18] ii. 193 n.   [19] ii. 514–19.

explained before the development of the aether theory, but then became clear:

> The periodic returns of so many diseases coincide with the diurnal, monthly, and annual rounds of time; that any one, who would deny the influence of the sun and moon on the periods of . . . fevers, must deny their effect on the tides, and on the seasons. . . . the fluid matter of gravitation permeates and covers all things, like the fluid matter of heat . . . (*Zoonomia*, ii. 510)

The existence of the word 'lunatic' in the language indicates how old the idea is,[20] but the most well-known and most disastrous lunar influence in literature may have been prompted by Darwin:

> One after one by the horned Moon
>   (Listen, O Stranger! to me)
> Each turn'd his face with a ghastly pang
>   And curs'd me with his ee.
>
> Four times fifty living men,
>   With never a sigh or groan,
> With heavy thump, a lifeless lump
>   They dropp'd down one by one . . .
>
> (*The Ancient Mariner*, 204–11)

The influence of eighteenth-century ideas on the active fluid of life is also evident later in Coleridge's poem:

> 'Marinere! thou hast thy will:
> For that, which comes out of thine eye, doth make
>   My body and soul to be still.'   (363–5)

In the last decades of the eighteenth century Dr Anton Mesmer became very wealthy and created much controversy in the capital cities of Europe. Translating the theory of aether into the medical sphere, Mesmer suggested that all living bodies were responsive to the movement of the universal fluid aether through them.[21] The influence of aether on animals he called 'animal magnetism', and

---

[20] Newton's doctor Richard Mead traced the old traditions in *De imperio Solis ac Lunae in Corpora Humana et Morbis inde oriundis* (1704) trans. Thomas Stack, *A Treatise Concerning the Influence of the Sun and Moon upon Human Bodies, and the Diseases thereby produced*, (1748). Mead noted that Aristotle had written that 'no animal dies but in the ebb of the tide' (p. 83).

[21] See F. A. Pattie, 'Mesmer's Medical Dissertation and Its Debt to Mead's *De Imperio Solis ac Lunae*', *J. Hist. Med.* xi (1956), 275–87.

suggested that if mankind could learn to control the fluid aether, health would be restored to those who, because of its imbalance, were suffering from disease.[22] From the late 1770s Mesmer's magnetic seances, often conducted with dozens of people at a time, were a fashionable part of life in Paris and London. Later, in the mid-1780s, animal magnetism became associated with political and religious radicalism and was discredited for offending against the sexual mores of the day.[23]

Something of this blend of mesmerism and radicalism is evident in Coleridge's pamphlet *An Answer to 'A Letter to Edward Long Fox, M.D.'*, which defended the Bristol radical physician from the accusation of dabbling in animal magnetism. Coleridge was, he professes, 'not surprised' at an attack on animal magnetism from a supporter of Pitt's government, and defended Fox's interest on the ground of free and unprejudiced inquiry, though showing little interest in the subject himself.[24] But Coleridge had not forgotten the work of the celebrated Bristol magnetist Dr de Mainauduc, who in the late 1780s magnetized patients, as Mesmer did, 'with his eyes, fixing his gaze on theirs':[25]

> And blest are they,
> Who in this fleshly World, the elect of Heaven,
> Their strong eye darting thro' the deeds of Men
> Adore with steadfast unpresuming gaze
> Him, Nature's Essence, Mind, and Energy!
>
> (*Religious Musings*, 51–5)

This passage matches in dramatic force and in meaning the lines in *The Ancient Mariner*, for the mariner is one of the elect of *Religious Musings* who impose their will on 'the deeds of Men' using 'Nature's

---

[22] *Mémoire sur la découverte du Magnétisme Animal* (1779); trans. V. R. Myers (London, 1948), 54–6.

[23] The magnetists' claims were investigated by a Royal Commission in 1784: *Report of Dr. Benjamin Franklin, and other Commissioners, charged by the King of France, with the Examination of the Animal Magnetism, as now practised at Paris* (1785). See R. Darnton, *Mesmerism and the End of the Enlightenment in France* (Cambridge, Mass., 1968), 3–45.

[24] *Lectures 1795*, 327–8. In an article on the popular millenarian prophet Richard Brothers in Apr. 1795, *The Times* had reported how the Revolution in France had been preceded by 'sects, mesmerists, somnambulists, prophets and prophetesses who had prepared the public mind for changes' (quoted in J. F. C. Harrison, *The Second Coming: Popular Millenarianism 1780–1850* (London, 1979), 76).

[25] A. Binet and C. Féré, *Animal Magnetism* (1887), 10.

Energy'. Caught by such a pure manifestation of the will of the deity in the elect being, the wedding guest is controlled 'body and soul'.[26]

Newton had wondered about the 'electric' nature of the universal causal agent in *Principia*, and between 1704 and 1713 he believed aether to be electrical, although he then became more cautious.[27] By the middle of the eighteenth century, however, an enormous number of electrical phenomena had been investigated. Among the extraordinarily diverse natural phenomena associated with the electric fluid was a 'living' electricity produced by marine animals such as electric eels and rays. An electric ray, the torpedo, attracted the most attention, and in 1773 and 1775 John Hunter published the results of his dissections of the torpedo and the *gymnotus* for the Royal Society.[28] As sea-luminescence was widely believed to be an electrical phenomenon, and many sea creatures were thought to arise spontaneously from sea-water, the presence of living electricity in the creatures strongly pointed to the electric fluid in the oceans as the source of the primordial power from which all life had originated.[29]

Benjamin Franklin's experiments to prove that lightning was electrical merely enhanced this view, for now electricity was seen in the depths and heights of nature. Newton's electric aether became the vital principal of the world, and, as John Wesley declared in *The Desideratum*, 'the Soul of the universe'.[30]

Evidently impressed with the power of the torpedo fish to numb its enemies, Coleridge referred to 'the torpedo touch of extreme Want' in *Conciones ad Populum*[31] and to 'the torpedo Touch of that Fiend' in a letter to George Dyer of March 1795.[32] Darwin had described the beneficial effects of electricity in promoting the germination of plants in 'The Economy of Vegetation', and the

---

[26] There are hints of animal magnetism and the power of the eye in *The Nightingale* and *Christabel*, part 1. These are probed in Beer, *Coleridge's Poetic Intelligence*, 220–6.

[27] J. E. McGuire, 'Force, Active Principles, and Newton's Invisible Realm', *Ambix*, xv (1968), 174–8.

[28] 'Anatomical Observations on the Torpedo', *Phil. Trans.* lxiii (1773), 481–9; 'An Account of the *Gymnotus Electricus*', ibid. lxv (1775), 395–407.

[29] Franklin initially believed that sea-luminescence was electrical, caused by friction between the water and passing ships. He changed his mind in a letter of 1753, quoted in E. N. Harvey, *A History of Luminescence: From the Earliest Times until 1900* (Philadelphia, Pa., 1957), 519–20.

[30] p. 9.   [31] *Lectures 1795*, 45.   [32] CL i. 155.

discovery that some higher plants gave out flashes of electricity was the subject of a footnote in 'The Loves of the Plants':

Miss E. C. Linneus first observed the tropaeolum Majus, to emit sparks or flashes in the mornings before sun-rise, during the months of June or July, and also during the twilight in the evening, but not after total darkness came on; these singular scintillations were shown to her father and other philosophers, and Mr. Wilcke, a celebrated electrician, believed them to be electric. . . . Nor is this more wonderful, than that the electric eel and torpedo should give voluntary shocks of electricity, and in this plant perhaps, as in those animals, it may be a mode of defence, by which it harasses or destroys the night-flying insects, which infest it . . . (iv. 45 n.)

At the end of this poem Darwin appended a note on the same phenomenon in the marigold plant, and Coleridge copied this as a footnote to his own 'Lines Written at Shurton Bars':

> 'Tis said, in Summer's evening hour
> Flashes the golden-colour'd flower
>   A fair electric flame.
> And so shall flash my love-charg'd eye
> When all the heart's big ecstacy
>   Shoots rapid thro' the frame!   (91–6)

Luigi Galvani had caused a stir in Europe by publishing a set of experiments in 1791 which seemed to prove that electricity was the vital principle in animals.[33] Attaching strips of dissimilar metals to limbs freshly cut from frogs, he had caused them to spasm by touching the metals together. Galvani's conclusion was that electricity was being discharged from within the limbs, and that this had been generated by the creature itself. 'Animal electricity' was produced from blood in the brain and passed from the head via nerves into muscles, which thus became charged. Motion was caused by the discharge of this electricity in the brain to the outside of the body, which stimulated the muscle-fibres to contract.

In 'Lines on a Friend who died of a frenzy fever' (1794), Coleridge wrote: 'Till FRENZY, fierce-ey'd child of moping pain, / Darts her hot lightning flash athwart the brain'. His image was taken from Darwin's report of the death of a famous Russian electrician, Richmann, who was killed in St Petersburg when lightning struck

---

[33] *De Viribus Electricitatis in motu musculari commentarius* trans. M. G. Foley, *Commentary on the Effects of Electricity on Muscular Motion* (Norwalk, Calif., 1953).

his head.[34] Yet Coleridge seems to know that the centre of animal electricity is in the brain, and confused Galvani's theory in his account of Hartley's work:

> and he of mortal kind
> Wisest, he* first who mark'd the ideal tribes
> Down the fine fibres from the sentient brain
> Roll subtly-surging.
>
> *DAVID HARTLEY
>
> (*Religious Musings*, 383–6)

This passage correctly describes 'animal electricity' which originates in the brain and passes *down* the nerves ('fine fibres') *to* the limbs, but it contradicts Hartley's theory of perception which describes how groups of ideas ('Ideal tribes') are propagated by vibrations *up* the nerves *to* the brain. Coleridge realized his mistake when revising the poem for the second edition, and corrected the passage to: 'he first who mark'd the ideal tribes / Up the fine fibres thro' the sentient brain.'[35]

As the various theories of the vital principle waxed and waned, attempts were made to unite them into some grand principle of life and motion in the universe. In *Dissertations on Different Subjects in Natural Philosophy* (1792) James Hutton suggested that the 'emanation of matter from the sun' was the 'necessary cause of vital motion', and that 'light, heat, and electricity, appear to be three different modifications of the same matter'.[36] The complexity of the imponderable fluids, active principles, and vital forces was difficult for those attempting to establish an order and economy to the system. Here the 19-year-old assistant to Thomas Beddoes at the Pneumatic Institution Humphry Davy discusses the vital principle in his first publication, 'An Essay on Heat, Light, and the Combinations of Light' (1799):

Is it not probable that the existence of some fine etherial principle on the brain and nerves is the immediate cause of sensible or perceptive action? If such a fluid exists, it must be continually supplied by the arterial blood, and constantly expended in sensible action. . . . Is it then improbable to suppose that LIGHT is attracted or secreted from the blood by the brain in

---

[34] 'Economy of Vegetation', i. 373 n.   [35] *Poems 1797*, 145.
[36] pp. 246, 263, 505–6.

the form of an etherial fluid or gas, and perpetually conveyed by the brain to the nerves?

A number of philosophers . . . have concluded the nervous fluid to be the electric aura. We have before supposed the electric fluid to be condensed light. Thus we have another cogent reason for supposing that the nervous spirit is light in an etherial gaseous form. (*The Collected Works of Sir Humphrey Davy, Bart.*, ed. John Davy, ii. (1839), 82)

Compared with such speculations, Coleridge's writings on the active principle of the natural world seem quite reasonable and restrained. In the opening passage of book II of *Joan of Arc* he suggests that these principles might seem to be distinct, but are all aspects of the one vital power in nature:

> Infinite myriads of self-conscious minds
> Form one all-conscious Spirit, who directs
> With absolute ubiquity of thought
> All his component monads, that yet seem
> With various province and apt agency
> Each to pursue its own self-centering end.   (44–9)

The poet continues by listing the spheres of activity in each of the elements of Earth ('mine'), Water ('juices'), Air ('clouds'), and Fire ('lightning'):

> Some nurse the infant diamond in the mine;
> Some roll the genial juices thro' the oak;
> Some drive the mutinous clouds to clash in air;
> And rushing on the storm with whirlwind speed
> Yoke the red lightning to their vollying car.
> Thus these pursue their never-varying course,
> No eddy in their stream.   (50–6)

In this passage are the seeds of the 'Hymns to the Elements' that Coleridge planned to write the following year.

Had Coleridge been asked in 1796 what it was about his band of elect beings that marked them out as representatives of God, he would have said that it was their imaginative faculty:

To develope the powers of the Creator is our proper employment — and to imitate Creativeness by combination our most exalted and self-satisfying Delight. But we are progressive and must not rest content with present Blessings. Our Almighty Parent hath therefore given to us Imagination that stimulates to the attainment of *real* excellence by the contemplation of splendid Possibilities that still revivifies the dying motive within us, and fixing our eye on the glittering Summits that rise one above the other in Alpine endlessness still urges us up the ascent of Being . . . (*Lectures 1795*, 235)

It is imagination which, according to Coleridge, urges us up the Great Chain of Being to perfect our nature. The idea does not originate with him. George Berkeley had expressed it fifty years earlier in his great Neoplatonic essay *Siris*:

Sense supplies images to memory. These become subjects for fancy to work upon. Reason considers and judges of the imaginations. And these acts of reason become new objects to the understanding. In this scale, each lower faculty is a step that leads to one above it. And the uppermost naturally leads to the deity, which is rather the object of intellectual knowledge . . . There runs a chain throughout the whole system of beings. In this chain one link drags another. (*Works* (1784), ii. 583–4)

In both Coleridge and Berkeley the increase of perceptive faculties is closely linked to the physical hierarchy in nature which was known as the Chain of Being: each part of nature was assigned to a particular step of existence which extended from the lowest inert matter through elementary plants and animals to the higher species—man, angels, and finally, the deity. Pope expressed this brilliantly in *An Essay on Man*:

> See, thro' this air, this ocean, and this earth,
> All matter quick, and bursting into birth.
> Above, how high, progressive life may go!
> Around, how wide! how deep extend below!
> Vast chain of Being, which from God began,
> Natures aethereal, human, angel, man,
> Beast, bird, fish, insect! what no eye can see,
> No glass can reach! from Infinite to thee,
> From thee to Nothing!—On superior pow'rs
> Were we to press, inferior might on ours:
> Or in the full creation leave a void,
> Where, one step broken, the great scale's destroy'd:
> From Nature's chain whatever link you strike,
> Tenth or ten thousandth, breaks the chain alike.   (233–46)

The Chain of Being was a familiar tenet of the Neoplatonist and it revived in the seventeenth century, when such ideas began to influence the leading naturalists of the day, each of whom attempted to show how, by origin and development, creatures achieve their level in the chain of existence.

William Harvey presented the classic essay of this school when he argued in *Anatomical Exercitations Concerning the Generation of Living Creatures* (1653) that for an animal to be conceived in the womb, there first must be a corresponding conception in the mind of the parents.[37] The psychic energy of the mind, transmitted from the male to the womb by way of the semen, would ignite the womb, and stimulate the egg to begin to grow. The imagination of the parents would act plastically to mould the form of the mature species on to the material of generation, thus causing the formation of a new individual. This power of the imagination of either parent to create the image of the new creature within the mother's womb was generally believed in the eighteenth century, and is well supported in literature. In a famous example, the opening chapter of Sterne's *The Life and Opinions of Tristram Shandy, Gentleman*, at the moment of Tristram's conception the imagination of his father is so disturbed by the mother's question about winding the clock that 'it scattered and dispersed the animal spirits' of the human foetus, laying a foundation for 'a thousand weaknesses both of body and mind, which no skill of the physician or the philosopher could ever afterwards have set thoroughly to rights'. But there were also reliably reported factual cases. A letter in the *Philosophical Transactions of The Royal Society* for 1687 gives an example of the effect of the mother's imagination:

One *Elizabeth Dooly* of the County of *Kilkenny* was aged 13 Years in *January* last: Her Mother being with Child of her was frighted by a Cow as she milked it, thrown down and hit on her Temple, within an eighth of an Inch of her Eye, by the Cow's Teat. This Child has exactly in that place, a piece of Flesh resembling a Cow's Teat, about 3 Inches and half in length: 'Tis very red, has a Bone in the midst about half the length of it; 'tis perforated and she Weeps through it; when she Laughs it wrincles up and contracts to two thirds of its length, and it grows in proportion to the rest of her Body. She is as sensible there as in any other part. This is lookt upon to be as strange an instant of the strength of Imagination as can be produced. (*Phil. Trans.* xvi (1686–92), 334)

Throughout the century the belief in the plastic creative power of the imagination remained strong. It was discussed in Richard

[37] See W. Pagel, *William Harvey's Biological Ideas* (New York, 1967), 271.

Sulivan's encyclopaedic *A View of Nature*, which Coleridge read in 1795:[38]

What is the probable account given by naturalists, of the marks of children in the womb from the imagination of the mother? . . . How do they explain the plastic power in the faetus, being within the plastic power of the mother, and being acted upon by the same spirit of nature? And what do they say to the strong and impulsive imagination of the mother, by a concurring action in the same plastic spirit in the faetus, affecting the tender and increasing parts of the faetus, and, like an impulsive signature, leaving the impression behind? (iii. 483–4)

Erasmus Darwin believed it was the male in the species, rather than the female, whose conceptions in the act of generation were paramount:

I conclude that the act of generation cannot exist without being accompanied with ideas, and that a man must have at that time either a general idea of his own male form, or of the form of his male organs; or an idea of the female form, or of her organs; and that this marks the sex, and the peculiar resemblances of the child to either parent. (*Zoonomia*, i. 524)

Yet if the imagination could influence the development and characteristics of individuals within a species, it could also aid the overall progress of the species to a higher state of being. Darwin saw the progressive or 'evolutionary' power of the imagination in the change and development of species:

The ingenious Dr. Hartley in his work on man, and some other philosophers, have been of opinion, that our immortal part acquires during this life certain habits of action or of sentiment, which become for ever indissoluble, continuing after death in a future state of existence; and add, that if these habits are of the malevolent kind, they must render the possessor miserable even in heaven. I would apply this ingenious idea to the generation or production of the embryon, or new animal, which partakes so much of the form and propensities of the parent. (ibid. i. 480)

In March 1810 Coleridge wrote in a notebook: 'I wish much to investigate the connection of the Imagination with the Bildungstrieb

---

[38] *A View of Nature, in Letters to a Traveller among the Alps*, 6 vols. (1794). Beer notes the influence of Sulivan on Coleridge (*Coleridge's Poetic Intelligence*, 46).

[generative principle] ... —Is not there a *link* between physical
Imitation & Imagination?'[39] In *The Friend* Coleridge equated the
'Bildungstrieb', which he had learned from study of Johann Blumenbach, with the vital principle of John Hunter, and so contradicted
his letter to Thelwall twelve years earlier.[40] Yet the connection
between imagination and generation occupied him to the end of his
life, and the Neoplatonic influence, mediated by Darwin and Sulivan,
undoubtedly fed his thoughts on what became the celebrated theory
of the primary imagination, the 'repetition in the finite mind of the
eternal act of creation'. At the heart of Coleridge's later theory of
the imagination is the conjunction of *creation* and *creativity* which
originates in the Platonic theory of Forms and permits the ideal
concept to become the realized, physical *conception*.

Before Coleridge, poets and philosophers had understood the
imagination merely as the 'image-making' faculty of the empiricists,
which represented the physical world to produce a world of light
and sound and beauty within the perception of man. The poet Mark
Akenside, writing in the preface to *The Pleasures of Imagination*
(1744) described the imagination as lying 'between the organs of
bodily sense and the faculties of moral perception', and so allowing
men to perceive more than mere physical sensation. But in the poem
he merely equates the imagination and the aesthetic faculty:

> On general habits, and on arts which grow
> Spontaneous in the minds of all mankind,
> Hath dwelt our argument; and how self-taught,
> Though seldom conscious of their own imploy,
> In nature's or in fortune's changeful scene
> Men learn to judge of beauty ...   (iv. 59–64)

Moreover, in spite of being praised by Darwin, Hartley could have
provided no clues to the activity of the imagination, for in *Observations on Man* it is merely the faculty which associates ideas of sense
to lead to the higher ideas of ambition, self-interest, sympathy,
theophany, and finally the moral sense. Only in the Neoplatonic
naturalist tradition would Coleridge have met the idea that the
imagination was the generative energy in man which prompted the
formation of the next, more perfect generation:

[39] CN iii. 3744.   [40] *The Friend*, i. 493.

> For Fancy is the power
> That first unsensualizes the dark mind
> Giving it new delights . . .
>
> (*Joan of Arc*, ii. 80–2)

> But soon Imagination conjur'd up
> An host of new desires . . .
>
> (*Religious Musings*, 215–16)

Our Almighty Parent hath therefore given to us Imagination that . . . urges us up the ascent of Being, amusing the ruggedness of the road with the beauty and grandeur of the ever-widening Prospect. (*Lectures 1795*, 235)

> Fancy now
> [Uprearing thro' the infinite of Truth *del.*]
> From these unmeasur'd and stupendous heights
> Fast-fluttering her vain pinions falls to earth
> And there lies panting . . .
>
> (Draft of *Religious Musings*: 'Rugby MS', fol. 57)

In this tradition the imagination is of the greatest importance as the creative power in man which forms throughout life new possibilities to be passed on to future generations.

The early conjunction of imagination and generation seems to have influenced Coleridge's great exposition of the creative spirit in man, the 'Letter to Sara Hutchinson'. Notice the link the poet makes between 'shaping' imagination and new generation:

> Ill Tidings bow me down to earth—
> Nor care I, that they rob me of my Mirth—
> But oh! each Visitation
> Suspends what Nature gave me at my Birth,
> My shaping Spirit of Imagination!   (238–42)

Later in the poem there is the famous passage on the imagination:

> O Sara! we receive but what we give,
> And in *our* Life alone does Nature live.
> Our's is her Wedding Garment, our's her Shroud—
> And would we aught behold of higher Worth
> Than that inanimate cold World allow'd
> To the poor loveless ever-anxious Crowd,
> Ah! from the Soul itself must issue forth
> A Light, a Glory, and a luminous Cloud
> Enveloping the Earth!   (296–304)

The 'Letter to Sara Hutchinson' is dated 4 April 1802. Seven weeks earlier Coleridge had got drunk:

> Feb. 14. 1802. Drank at Bellows a glass of wine, & 2 pretty large Beakers of Punch — in high spirits — went to bed. A luminous cloud interposed between my Limbs & the sheet — wherever I drew a figure with my nail on my leg or thigh, the same *appeared* in my limb & all, the path of the nail a luminous white, like phosphorus in oxygen, or the falls which we made in the water in Wales. When I press my thigh a great luminous Mist of White burst out of the spectrum Thigh. (*CN* i. 1108)

This experience was important for Coleridge. Perhaps he believed that he had actually witnessed his vital principle, the primary creative imagination. In the 'Letter to Sara' he made the 'luminous cloud' into a life-giving force, like the 'intellectual Breeze' of 'The Eolian Harp'. This experience remained with him for many years, and in a letter to Thomas Boosey, jun. of May 1817 Coleridge retold it in a discussion of another of the active fluids in nature, animal magnetism.[41]

At the time of his drinking-bout at Bellows's, Coleridge was an attentive student at Humphry Davy's chemical lectures at the Royal Institution, where the young lecturer was introducing the new chemistry to a fashionable audience with beautiful and spectacular demonstrations. Coleridge described these vividly in his notebook, and included a note on the luminescent element phosphorus, which Davy burnt in air: 'Oxygen Gas separated from Nitrogene by Phosphorus, which rapidly combines with the Oxygen & forms Phos. Acid'.[42] Why, after his drinking-bout, Coleridge should associate

---

[41] *CL* iv. 730–1. Coleridge associated animal magnetism with the imagination in a late notebook entry: 'if the zoö-magnetic influx be only the influence of the Imagination, the active Imagination may be a form of the Zoö-magnetic Influence' (N. 29, fol. 62); quoted in T. H. Levere, 'S. T. Coleridge and the Human Sciences: Anthropology, Phrenology, and Mesmerism', in M. P. Hanen, M. J. Osler, and R. G. Weyant (eds.), *Science, Pseudo-Science and Society* (Waterloo, NY, 1980), 187.

[42] *CN* i. 1098. In 'Coleridge: A Bridge between Science and Poetry' (in J. Beer (ed.), *Coleridge's Variety: Bicentenary Studies* (London, 1974), 81–100) Kathleen Coburn pointed to the infamy of the common elision in Coleridge's letter to Davy of May 1801: 'chemistry . . . is saying nothing'. The full passage reads: 'I am perpetually saying — probably, there are many agents hitherto undiscovered. This cannot be *reasoning*; for in all conclusive reasoning we must have a deep conviction that all the *terms* have been exhausted. This is saying no more than that (with Dr Beddoes's

the luminous cloud which rose from his limbs with the burning of
'phosphorus in oxygen' and with moving water, will be the strange
subject of the final chapter of this book.

leave) chemistry can never possess the same degree of certainty with mathematics —
in truth, it is saying nothing' (*CL* ii. 727).

8

Poetry of Generation and Decay

All Birds, Beasts and Fishes, Insects, Trees, and other Vegetables,
with their several Parts, grow out of Water and watry Tinc-
tures and Salts, and by Putrefaction return again into watry
substances.

Newton, Opticks (1717–18)

IN 1677 in Dresden, Johann Kunckel isolated the element phosphorus
from human urine and wondered at his new substance as it glowed
with cold light in the dark. Four years later John Evelyn marvelled
at the new substance when it was demonstrated at the Royal
Society.[1] '[C]omposed of Urine & humane bloud,' the diarist
recorded, 'which gives greate light to Dr. *Willis* &c notions of the
flamula Vitalis which animates the bloud, & is, for ought we know,
the animal life it selfe of all things living.'[2] This curious property
of glowing without heat suggested to early observers and investigators
that phosphorus was different in kind from other materials. As it
could only be obtained from urine, the notion grew that it might
be the very 'flame of life' itself. Berkeley recorded this belief in *Siris*:

> That there is really such a thing as vital flame, actually kindled, nourished
> and extinguished like common flame, and by the same means, is an opinion
> of some moderns, particularly of Dr. Willis in his tract De Sanguinis
> Accensione . . . and perhaps there may be some truth in this, if it be so
> understood, as that light or fire might indeed constitute the animal spirit
> or immediate vehicle of the soul. (*Works* (1784), ii. 555–6)

'The Alchymst, in search of the Philosopher's Stone, discovers
Phosphorus', painted by Joseph Wright of Derby in 1771, succinctly
records the optimism of a century in which it was believed the
processes of life were now being revealed to mankind.

Not until the 1780s, when Anton Lavoisier burnt it in air and
formed an inorganic acid, did phosphorus lose its special place
between inert matter and living things. Lavoisier's work on the

---

[1] See D. M. Knight, 'The Vital Flame', *Ambix*. xxiii (1976), 5.
[2] *The Diary of John Evelyn*, ed. E. S. De Beer, 6 vols. (Oxford, 1955), iv.
252.

burning of phosphorus did not, however, stop the huge fascination with the phenomenon which phosphorus displays and to which it owes its name: phosphorescence.

> The very deeps did rot: O Christ!
>   That ever this should be!
> Yea, slimy things did crawl with legs
>   Upon the slimy Sea.
>
> About, about, in reel and rout
>   The Death-fires danc'd at night;
> The water, like a witch's oils,
>   Burnt green and blue and white.
>
> (*The Ancient Mariner*, 119–26)

The Ancient Mariner is a poem about a man who kills a friendly sea-bird and is cursed to watch the death of the natural order around him. His shipmates die; every living thing in the stagnant ocean dies. The ocean decays and out of it, spontaneously generated from the putrescence, insects grow. Now the sea-water becomes luminescent and for seven days and seven nights the ocean rots and only the mariner and the parasitic insects live on in the dying world, lit by the mysterious light in the water. Yet after the curse has ended and a new creative act forms life once more in the ocean, it is once again luminescent light which shines from the joyful, vital scene:

> The moving Moon went up the sky
>   And no where did abide:
> Softly she was going up
>   And a star or two beside—
>
> Her beams bemock'd the sultry main
>   Like morning frosts yspread;
> But where the ship's huge shadow lay,
> The charmed water burnt alway
>   A still and awful red.
>
> Beyond the shadow of the ship
>   I watch'd the water-snakes:
> They mov'd in tracks of shining white;
> And when they rear'd, the elfish light
>   Fell off in hoary flakes.

> Within the shadow of the ship
>   I watch'd their rich attire:
> Blue, glossy green, and velvet black
> They coil'd and swam; and every track
>   Was a flash of gold fire.

(ibid. 255–73)

In the last chapter the connection was established between imagination and generation in Coleridge's thought, and the poet's association of imagination and the vital spirit were also noted. In this chapter I wish to develop these ideas further, by suggesting that the central imagery of *The Ancient Mariner*, and an earlier passage in the second book of *Joan of Arc* gains strength when the link is made between the phenomenon of luminescence and the vital principle.

All animate and inanimate bodies which emit light without the accompanying emission of heat are known as *luminescents*. The energy which produces this light may have been gained previously by absorption from the sun, or may be generated as the result of an internal chemical or biochemical change in the material itself. The first type of luminescence is known as phosphorescence and is a property of some inorganic bodies; light-emission by chemical or biological changes is called chemiluminescence or bioluminescence and is a feature of many substances and living beings. Curiously, phosphorus itself is a chemiluminescent, and emits light by reacting slowly with oxygen in the atmosphere.

Interest in luminescence pre-dates Aristotle, who noted the light of fungi, dead fish, the *aurora borealis*, and sea-luminescence. Modern investigation of the phenomena began in 1610 when the first artificial phosphorescent material, known as the Bologna stone, was prepared in Italy. Many philosophers, including Galileo and Boyle, became interested in luminescence, and by the end of the seventeenth century many real and imagined luminescents had been described. Of particular interest were the observations made of light which came from the sea:

And when I remember how many questions I have asked navigators about the luminousness of the sea; and how in some places the sea is wont to shine in the night as far as the eye can reach; at other times and places, only when the waves dash against the vessel, or the oars strike and cleave the water; how some seas shine often, and other[s] have not been observed to shine; how in some places the sea has been taken notice of to shine when such and such winds blow, whereas in other seas, the observation holds not; and in the same tract of sea, within a narrow compass, one part of the water will be luminous, whilst the other shines not at all. (*Works of the Honourable Robert Boyle* (1772), iii. 231)

As interest in luminescence grew and the number of known luminescents increased, attempts were made to classify them according to whether their light was produced spontaneously, or only after being stimulated. The former were called 'natural phosphors', and included living creatures such as glow-worms and fireflies, rotting matter (commonly flesh, wood, and fish); and the uniform glowing of the sea noted by Boyle. 'Artificial phosphors' were the several inorganic phosphors and the sea-water which sparkled when creatures or ships passed through it.

Above all it was sea-light which fascinated and mystified seafarers, and reports of the phenomenon became so numerous in the early part of the eighteenth century that the French Academy of Sciences took the odd step of publishing a warning to the public against reading sensationalized accounts.[3] The dull red 'burning of the sea' only visible in a calm was contrasted with the brighter blue-white light seen when sea-water was agitated by ships or in a storm. Many prizes were offered for an explanation of the phenomena, but no satisfactory theory was forthcoming: although superficial examination showed that brighter flashes in sea-water were caused by small jelly-like creatures known as medusae, no one before the late nineteenth century saw the myriads of microscopic animals which actually produce the uniform light. In fact, sea-luminescence is always blue-white, and the uniform dull red 'burning of the sea' and the 'red tides', which Coleridge described as 'still and awful red' in *The Ancient Mariner*, are not luminescences, but sudden blooms of red plankton.

A significant advance in the investigation of bioluminescence was made during James Cook's voyage round the world in the years 1772–5 when, on the night of 29 October 1772 off the Cape of Good Hope, the crew of the *Resolution*, including Coleridge's future teacher the astronomer William Wales,[4] saw a vividly luminescent sea:

---

[3] Harvey, *History of Luminescence*, 518. My chapter is indebted to this study.
[4] See B. Smith, 'Coleridge's *Ancient Mariner* and Cook's Second Voyage', *J. Warburg & Courtauld Inst.* xix (1956), 117–54.

The night was scarcely begun, when the water all round us afforded the most grand and astonishing sight that can be imagined. As far as we could see the whole ocean seemed to be in a blaze. Every breaking wave had its summit illuminated by a light similar to that of phosphorus, and the sides of the vessel, coming in contact with the sea, were strongly marked by a luminous line. Great bodies of light moved in the water along our side, sometimes slower, sometimes quicker; now in the same direction with our course, now flying off from it; sometimes we could clearly distinguish their shape to be that of fishes, which when they approached any smaller ones, forced these to hasten away from them. (George Forster, *A Voyage round the World* (etc.), 2 vols. (1777), i. 54–5)

The two naturalists on board the *Resolution*, Johann Forster and his son Georg, drew buckets of the luminescent water on to the deck; on examination it was found to be full of small creatures resembling bits of jelly. When the buckets were stirred, the creatures shone brightly:

After the water had been standing for a little while, the small sparkling objects seemed to decrease in quantity, but, by stirring the water again, we observed the whole to be again entirely luminous; and leaving the water undisturbed, we saw the little sparks moving very briskly in different directions. Though the bucket with the water was suspended, that it might be less affected by the motion of the ship, the sparkling objects still moved to and fro', so that this first convinced me, that these luminous atoms had a voluntary motion, quite independent of the agitation of the water or the ship; but, at each agitation of the water by a stick or the hand, we plainly perceived the sparkling to increase. (John Reinold Forster, *Observations made during a voyage round the World* (1778), 64)

The idea that the light of the sea was organic rather than mechanical had been advanced at the beginning of the century by a Jesuit missionary, Father Bourzes, who observed a remarkable luminescence in the Indian Ocean on 10 July 1704, caused, he believed, by the 'fat and glutinous'[5] quality of the sea in that region. However, the simple experiments on the deck of the *Resolution* are important as one of the first proofs that sea-luminescence is caused by 'animalcules' (i.e. protozoa) which give out light when they are agitated.[6]

---

[5] 'A letter from Father *Bourzes* to Father *Estienne Souciet*, concerning the *Luminous Appearance* observable in the *Wakes* of *Ships* in the *Indian* Seas', *Phil. Trans.* xxviii (1713), 234.

[6] The Forsters probably examined the luminous protozoa *Noctiluca militaris*, the largest of the marine flagellates.

Johann Forster was intrigued by the phenomenon of sea-luminescence and speculated on its possible causes, thinking that different appearances of sea-light required different explanations. He suggested that the dull red 'burning' of the ocean, visible in calm seas, and contrasting sharply with the bright blue light of agitated water, was not caused by living creatures, but came from the putrefaction of fish and moluscs in stagnant seas:

It is likewise a well established fact, that the ocean, itself after a long continued calm, becomes stinking and highly putrid, arising probably from the putrefaction of a great many animal substances, that die in the ocean, float in it, and in hot calm days frequently and suddenly putrefy. That fishes and mollusca contain oily and inflammable particles is equally well known. The acid of phosphorus disengaged by putrefaction from its original mixture in animal bodies, may easily combine with some of the just mentioned inflammables, and thus produce a phosphorus floating on the top of the ocean, and causing that luminous appearance, which we so much admire. (*Observations made during a voyage,* 66–7)

This explanation, which makes phosphorus so important to the processes of life, was taken from Joseph Priestley's discussion of luminescence in *The History and Present State of Discoveries relating to Vision, Light, and Colours* (1772). In a chapter titled 'Of light proceeding from Putrescent Substances, &c. and Phosphorus' Priestley described the observations of Father Bourzes in the 'fatty' Indian Ocean, and concluded that Bourzes's description made it 'extremely probable that the luminousness of the sea arises from slimy and other putrescent matter with which it abounds'.[7] Priestley was unsure what the putrescent material was, but noted the similarity of its light to that of phosphorus:

A light in some respects similar to that of putrescent matter has been found to proceed from that celebrated chymical production called *phosphorus*, which is, in fact, an *imperfect sulphur*, tending to decompose itself, and so as to take fire by the access of *air* only. Phosphorus, therefore, when it emits light is properly a *body ignited*; though when a very small quantity of it is used . . . the heat is not sensible. But perhaps the matter which emits the light in what we call *putrescent substances* may be similar to it, though it be generated by a different process, and burn with a less degree of heat. (*History and Present State,* ii. 584)

[7] ii. 576.

Although these ideas are speculative and pre-date Priestley's chemical research, he was one of the first writers to realize that phosphorus emits light by slow combustion, and to understand the importance of the phenomenon of luminescence for organic matter. For a century phosphorus had been connected with the flame of life, and its light had been a manifestation of life. Even after Lavoisier's work on combustion, phosphorus retained its association with the fundamental process of life, as Darwin here makes clear:

As animal respiration seems to be a kind of slow combustion, in which it is probable that phosphoric acid is produced by the union of phosphorus with the vital air, so it is also probable that phosphoric acid is produced . . . in the excretory or respiratory vessels of luminous insects, as the glow-worm and fire-fly, and some marine insects. ('Economy of Vegetation', add. n. X)

After Priestley's work it could also be associated with death and decay:

From the same principle I suppose the light from putrid fish, as from the heads of hadocks, and from putrid veal, and from rotten wood in a certain state of their putrefaction, is produced, and phosphorus thus slowly combined with air is changed into phosphoric acid. (ibid.)

Thus in the 1780s and 1790s luminescence became an important manifestation of the processes of life and death. When animals breathe, phosphorus in their bodies is changed into phosphoric acid and light is produced. When they die and their bodies begin to decay, phosphorus is released in oils, and light is produced as this putrid oil is exposed to air.

This could now explain the diversity of sea-luminescences: in rough seas, or in the wakes of ships, sea creatures move in water that has plenty of fresh oxygen and they are agitated to give out light as a result of the turbulence in the water. In calm torrid seas the lack of oxygen in the water kills them, and as their bodies putrefy light is again produced. Sea-luminescence was, for the natural philosopher, a phenomenon of life and death.

The decaying, burning sea of *The Ancient Mariner* had been anticipated in three lines that occur at the end of Coleridge's passage from the second book of *Joan of Arc*:

Shriek'd AMBITION's ghastly throng,
And with them those, the locust Fiends that crawl'd
And glitter'd in CORRUPTION's slimy track.   (ii. 420-2)

The Ancient Mariner also describes how 'The very deeps did rot' and the water became 'slimy' as tiny creatures grew from the putrefying ocean and the sea burned. Yet unlike the early poem, life is suddenly formed out of the dead ocean. Sea-snakes swim exuberantly through the water, and flash with fire; they agitate the sea and form 'tracks of shining white' which at length invade the darkness around the ship and break the curse.

When Coleridge wrote *The Ancient Mariner*, he had never been to sea. Not until several months after the publication of *Lyrical Ballads* in 1798 did he take the packet from Harwich, and experience the phenomenon he had written about:

The Ocean is a noble Thing by night; a beautiful white cloud of foam at momently intervals roars & rushes by the side of the Vessel, and Stars of Flame dance & sparkle & go out in it — & every now and then light Detachments of Foam dart away from the Vessel's side with their galaxies of stars, & scour out of sight, like a Tartar Troop over a Wilderness! — What these Stars are, I cannot say — the sailors say, that they are the Fish Spawn which is phosphorescent. (letter to Sara Coleridge, 18 September 1798; *CL* i. 416)

The sailors who informed the poet of the cause of the 'galaxies of stars' in the ocean were probably long dead, for in Father Bourzes's account of the luminescent sea in the Indian Ocean there occurs this passage:

Besides, in sailing over some Places of the Sea, we find a Matter or Substance of different Colours, sometimes red, sometimes yellow. In looking at it, one would think it was Saw-dust: Our Sailors say it is the Spawn or Seed of Whales. What it is, is not certain; but when we draw up Water in passing over these Places, it is always viscous and glutinous. Our Mariners also say, that there are a great many heaps or Banks of this Spawn in the North; and that sometimes in the Night they appear all over of a bright Light, without being put in Motion by any Vessel or Fish passing by them. ('Letter from Father Bourzes', 234)

The attribution of luminescent properties to the spawn or seed of sea creatures is significant. When the ocean begins to decay in *The Ancient Mariner* 'slimy things' appear, giving that 'glutinous' quality noted by Bourzes. Eventually these become the young forms of sea-snakes, but as they first appear they seem to the mariner to be generated spontaneously from the rotting organic matter of the ocean.

In the eighteenth century many types of living beings were believed to rise spontaneously, either from inorganic matter or from putrefying organic remains. Blake drew on the idea in the final book of *Vala; or the Four Zoas* (1797–1800):

> For lo! the winter melted away upon the distant hills,
> And all the black mould sings. She speaks to her infant race, her milk
> Descends down on the sand; the thirsty sand drinks & rejoices,
> Wondering to behold the emmet, the grasshopper, the jointed worm;
> The roots shoot thick through the solid rocks, bursting their way;
> They cry out in joys of existence. The broad stems
> Rear on the mountain stem after stem, the scaly newt creeps
> From the stone & the armed fly springs from the rocky crevice.
> The spider, the bat burst from the hardened slime crying
> To one another, 'What are we, & whence is our joy & delight?'
>
> (ix. 597–606)

This was the age in which theories of generation were keenly debated, for many believed that by denying the necessity of a creative act in the process of generation, spontaneous generation cast serious and unacceptable doubts on God's creative activity in the world. Hence the extraordinary theory of pre-existence or *evolution* had been developed, which denied all types of new generation whatsoever, and argued that

the germ of every animal, and every plant that ever has lived and ever will live, were all created at one and the same time, namely, at the beginning of the world; and that all that is necessary is, that one generation should be developed after the other. (Johann Blumenbach, *Über den Bildungstrieb das Zeugungsgeschäfte* (Göttingen, 1781), sect. 1; trans. Andrew Crichton, *An Essay on Generation* (London [1792]), 5.

The central dogmatic belief of this theory is that as God created all things in six days, there can be no new creation in the world, and the creation of genuine new life in species is thus impossible. The proponents of the theory of evolution suggested that the germs of all the creatures that had existed since the Creation and are to live before the end of time were contained, each within the other, in the first womb, like an unending series of Russian dolls. Although naturalists disputed whether the male or female of the species was the guardian of these primordial germs of life, most believed that the female 'hosted' the foetus, which began to develop after being supplied with the energy for growth by the male.

Spermatozoa were seen in male fluid in the late seventeenth century, but the tiny animalcules were not considered by many to be relevant to the process of generation. Lazaro Spallanzani, the great Italian naturalist whose work was translated by Beddoes in 1784, performed experiments in the 1740s to prove the irrelevance of these animalcules in semen; destroying all the 'worms' in the sperm of several species of frog and toad he still succeeded in obtaining fertilized eggs.[8]

Even those who could not accept the strange consequences of the theory of evolution did not accept that the microscopic worms seen in the male fluid were necessary for the process of generation. These naturalists, who numbered among them Blumenbach and Darwin, thought they were spontaneously generated worms:

> . . . I cannot conceive how some professed philosophers, and natural historians have been led to deny life and voluntary motion to those animalculae; but I am still more at a loss to imagine, how another set of philosophers have been induced to dignify these animalculae of a stagnant animal fluid, to the high rank of the organized germs of successive generations. (Blumenbach, *Essay on Generation*, trans. Crichton, 8–9)

The 'spermists' in fact were very few, for those who believed that the rudiments of the foetus were generated in the male and passed to the nutritive womb of the female did not usually identify this tiny 'homuncule' with the microscopic worms. If not spontaneously generated in old fluid, they could be thought to be parasites, passed on from generation to generation as agents of God's punishment at the Fall.[9] Erasmus Darwin believed in a 'filament of life', but did not identify this with the spermatozoa, which he thought were artefacts. 'I do not assert that these moving particles, visible by the microscope, are homunciones,' he wrote in *Zoonomia*; 'perhaps they may be the creatures of stagnation or putridity, or perhaps no creatures at all.'[10]

---

[8] *Dissertazioni di fisica animale e vegetabile* (1780); trans. Thomas Beddoes, *Dissertations relative to the Natural History of Animals and Vegetables*, 2nd edn., 2 vols. (1789), ii. 72–5, 177–85.

[9] See J. Farley, *The Spontaneous Generation Controversy from Descartes to Operin* (Baltimore, Md., 1977), ch. 1.

[10] i. 484–5.

Darwin had endorsed the spontaneous generation theory three years
earlier in 'The Economy of Vegetation':

> GNOMES! with nice eye the slow solution watch,
> With fostering hand the parting atoms catch,
> Join in new forms, combine with life and sense,
> And guide and guard the transmigrating Ens . . .   (ii. 581–4)

These lines, he explained in a footnote, refer to 'the short time in
which the recrements of animal or vegetable bodies become again
vivified in the forms of vegetable mucor or microscopic insects'.
Interestingly, a long note[11] in Darwin's final work *The Temple of
Nature; or, the Origin of Society* published posthumously in 1803
defended the theory of spontaneous generation, and provoked a
paper from his old exiled friend Joseph Priestley, whose 'Observations
and Experiments relating to Equivocal or Spontaneous Generation'
was published after his own death in 1806.[12] It was an ironic choice
of subject for moribund disagreement.

Coleridge's first reference to the phenomenon of primal generation
is his Miltonic allegory of the Creation and the origin of evil in *Joan
of Arc*. This passage is so crowded that even its author had trouble
with it, writing on a copy of the poem in 1814: 'These are very fine
Lines, tho' I say it, that should not: but hang me, if I know or ever
did know the meaning of them, tho' my own composition':[13]

> Of CHAOS the adventurous progeny
> Thou seest; foul missionaries of foul sire,
> Fierce to regain the losses of that hour
> When LOVE rose glittering, and his gorgeous wings
> Over the abyss flutter'd with such glad noise,
> As what time after long and pestful Calms
> With slimy shapes and miscreated life
> Pois'ning the vast Pacific, the fresh breeze
> Wakens the merchant sail, uprising. NIGHT
> An heavy unimaginable moan
> Sent forth, when she the PROTOPLAST beheld
> Stand beauteous on Confusion's charmed wave.   (ii. 225–36)

---

[11] Add. n., 'Spontaneous Vitality of Microscopic Animals', pp. 1–11.
[12] *Trans. Amer. Phil. Soc.* vi (1806), 119–26.
[13] Marginalia transcribed by E. H. Coleridge in *Complete Poetical Works*, i.
140 n.

The primary image is the Spirit of God brooding over the waters of chaos in the seventh book of *Paradise Lost*; but it is a muted Creation that Coleridge presents, for instead of the brilliant invigorating light that destroys the darkness in Genesis the poetry describes a fluttering, glittering spirit, which hovers without power, and evokes in the reader a world of secondary powers and shadowy forms.

The poetry compares this creative act to that of a sea-breeze which, by driving a becalmed ship through the ocean, generates new and glittering life in its wake. Coleridge's simile seems to originate in a note 'Luminous Insects' from 'The Economy of Vegetation':

> In some seas, as particularly about the coast of Malabar, as a ship floats along, it seems during the night to be surrounded with fire, and to leave a long tract of light behind it. . . . As numerous microscopic insects are found in this shining water, its light has been generally ascribed to them, though it seems probable that fish-slime in hot countries may become in such a state of incipient putrefaction as to give light, especially when by agitation it is more exposed to the air . . . (Add. n. IX)

In *Joan of Arc* this glittering wake of a ship became the manifestation of new life in the ocean, the creation by the first being, the Protoplast.

Coleridge's use of this word is interesting. It is first recorded in his 1795 notebook,[14] where he may have transcribed from Newton's famous letter to Henry Oldenburg of December 1695:

> *the frame of nature may be nothing but aether condensed by a fermental principle* . . . wrought into various forms, at first by the immediate hand of the Creator, and ever since by the power of nature, who by virtue of the command, *Increase and multiply*, became a complete imitator of the copies set her by the Protoplast. (in *Works of the Honourable Robert Boyle (1772), i. p. cxviii*)

Yet the closest parallel to the Protoplast in *Joan of Arc* is not Newton's distant Demi-Urge, but the 'intellectual Breeze' of 'The Eolian Harp', which sweeps through nature as an immanent inspirational power, animating the world of dull matter. In *Joan of Arc* the fresh breeze brings life to a lifeless ocean, and the 'Protoplast' demonstrates the internal formative energy of the deity which is so intimately bound to nature.

---

[14] *CN* i. 40, which is the 3rd recorded use in the *OED*, the 2 previous being du Wes *c.*1532, and Watson in *Decacordon* (1602): 'In Salem . . . was Adam our protoplast created.'

Until the creative power of nature wakens it the ocean in *Joan of Arc*, like stagnant male fluid, is full of 'slimy shapes and miscreated life', the chance, spontaneous generations of a decaying world. But although corrupted, the water is a potentially generative seminal fluid, and needs only the energy of plastic nature to activate it. The Spirit of God rising over the waters of chaos does this, and life is produced from the lifeless sea:

> When LOVE rose glittering, and his gorgeous wings
> Over the abyss flutter'd with such glad noise,
> As what time after long and pestful Calms
> With slimy shapes and miscreated life
> Pois'ning the vast Pacific, the fresh breeze
> Wakens the merchant sail, uprising.   (ii. 228–33)

This allegory, with its clear phallic reference in the final line, accurately parallels the procreative act in man; for the stagnant fluid in which worms grow spontaneously only becomes a living generative fluid when, in a moment of creative imagination, the male acts plastically to conceive new life.

The ocean in *Joan of Arc* is thus the primal fluid out of which all life began. In this sea, as in the male fluid, creatures may arise spontaneously amid decay and corruption; or may grow with vital forms as the plastic Spirit of God moves over the waters:

> Of CHAOS the adventurous progeny
> Thou seest; foul missionaries of foul sire,
> Fierce to regain the losses of that hour
> When LOVE rose glittering . . .
>
>   . . . . . .
>
>   NIGHT
> An heavy unimaginable moan
> Sent forth, when she the PROTOPLAST beheld
> Stand beauteous on Confusion's charmed wave.
>   (ii. 225–8, 233–6)

In *Joan of Arc* a ship is becalmed on a sea which is poisoned with slimy shapes and miscreated life; the creatures glitter amid the corruption and are dispelled by the formation of new life in the water by a breeze which is an agent of the creative power of God.

In *The Ancient Mariner* a ship is becalmed on a silent ocean which rots and generates slimy things among fires of decay. These creatures live in the corruption until they are dispelled by the rising moon, whose light reveals new and vital forms in the ocean.

In both *Joan of Arc* and *The Ancient Mariner* luminescence describes both decay and generation, and death and renewal occur under the 'cold light' of the moon. But in *The Ancient Mariner* the agent of the creative love of God became his angel of death. Coleridge's prose poem 'The Wanderings of Cain', written in November 1797, posed the question through Cain:

Who is the God of the dead? where doth he make his dwelling? what sacrifices are acceptable unto him? for I have offered, but have not been received; I have prayed, and have not been heard; and how can I be afflicted more than I already am? (174–9)

The central stanzas of *The Ancient Mariner* answer this question. The God of the living is the God of the dead. The light of the moon is a creative and a destructive power; and luminescence, the sign of beauty and life, is also the sign of corruption and decay. God destroys the life he creates:

> The many men so beautiful,
>   And they all dead did lie!
> And a million million slimy things
>   Liv'd on—and so did I.
>
> I look'd upon the rotting Sea,
>   And drew my eyes away;
> I look'd upon the eldritch deck,
>   And there the dead men lay.   (228–35)

For 'seven days, seven nights', the time God took to create the world in the beginning, the mariner exists, the sole survivor among the corruption of the old world. No new creative act occurs. In the chaos of this degenerate, primeval world he sees the inevitability of the cycle of life, death, and rebirth that is the mode of God's creative action in the world. The sign of this knowledge, the glittering eye of Coleridge's elect beings, is the mark of the cursed mariner's power and knowledge.

The strength and economy of the lines in the poem that portray the decay of the ocean are readily seen once they are juxtaposed with short passages from Coleridge's reading:

> The very deeps did rot: O Christ!
> That ever this should be!
> Yea, slimy things did crawl with legs
> Upon the slimy Sea. (119–22)

It is likewise a well established fact, that the ocean, itself after a long continued calm, becomes stinking and highly putrid . . . (J. Forster, *Observations made during a voyage*, 66)

During a calm, on the morning of the 2d, some parts of the sea seemed covered with a kind of slime; and some small sea animals were swimming about. The most conspicuous of which, were of the gelatinous, or *medusa* kind . . . (James Cook and James King, *A Voyage to the Pacific Ocean*, 3 vols (1784) ii. 257)

Our Sailors say it is the Spawn or Seed of Whales. . . . when we draw up Water in passing over these Places, it is always viscous and glutinous. ('Letter from Father Bourzes', 234)

I do not assert that these moving particles, visible by the microscope, are homunciones; perhaps they may be the creatures of stagnation or putridity. (Darwin, *Zoonomia*, i. 484–5)

And with them those, the locust Fiends that crawl'd / And glitter'd in CORRUPTION's slimy tract. (Coleridge, *Joan of Arc*, ii. 421–2)

> About, about, in reel and rout
> The Death-fires danc'd at night;
> The water, like a witch's oils,
> Burnt green and blue and white. (123–6)

[A] great many animal substances . . . die in the ocean, float in it, and in hot calm days frequently and suddenly putrefy. That fishes and mollusca contain oily and inflammable particles is equally well known. (Forster, *Observations*, 67)

I suppose the light from putrid fish . . . in a certain state of their putrefaction, is produced, and phosphorus thus slowly combined with air is changed into phosphoric acid. (Darwin, 'Economy of Vegetation', add. n. X).

Phosphorus, therefore, when it emits light is properly a *body ignited* . . . perhaps the matter which emits the light in what we call *putrescent substances* may be similar to it. (Priestley, *History and Present State*, ii. 584)

If one takes some Water out of the Sea, and stirs it never so little with his Hand in the dark, he may see in it an infinite number of bright Particles. The Production of this Light depends very much on the Quality of the Water . . . the Light is largest when the Water is fattest and fullest of Foam . . . and Linnen moisten'd with it produced a great deal of Light, if it were stir'd or mov'd briskly. ('Letter from Father Bourzes', 233–4)

But, with candle light, the colour was, chiefly, a beautiful, pale green, tinged with a burnished gloss; and, in the dark, it had a faint appearance of glowing fire. (Cook and King, *Voyage to Pacific*, ii. 257)

By killing the albatross the mariner destroyed the bearer of God's creative power in the world, and so usurped divine activity. He is cursed to endure the loneliness of a world without life, in the primeval state before life was created. Instead of exulting in his Godlike position, the mariner can think only of the opportunistic creatures that have arisen spontaneously from the corruption. Like them, his life continues parasitically: they feed on death in the ocean, he lives at the cost of his fellows:

> The many men so beautiful,
>   And they all dead did lie!
> And a million million slimy things
>   Liv'd on—and so did I.   (228–31)

All things end in death and corruption, for life is generated from death and feeds upon it. The 'economy of nature', the finest achievement of natural philosophy in the latter half of the eighteenth century and the great celebration of God's interest and involvement in the world, was finally revealed in its true horror:

All animals derive their existence from a watery or slimy substance, nourished by other aqueous and succulent substances in the womb, which by the natural alchymy, is changed into flesh, blood, skin, bones, &c. Do not they return to what they sprung from, a slimy, glutinous liquid? (Sulivan, *A View of Nature*, iii. 496–7)

Thus suspended between the death of the old world and the birth of the new, the mariner can only see the terrible inevitability of decay and corruption that is the end of all things:

> I look'd upon the rotting Sea,
>   And drew my eyes away;
> I look'd upon the eldritch deck,
>   And there the dead men lay.   (232–5)

A tale like *The Ancient Mariner* is perhaps not surprising from one of that generation who lived in the age when the *ancien régime* was purged from Europe. Like the mariner in the poem, many of the young radicals felt that they had been born between two worlds, and that they were denied entry to both. They had known little other than the bloody European conflict that marked the end of the old world. '[T]he present generation will appear to the future as the Adam of a new world', Paine had written in 1790.[15] Before this new world, a cleansing apocalypse had swept through the nations. Thus *The Ancient Mariner* is set in an apocalyptic age.

Coleridge knew from Burnet the events that were to occur in the latter days of the world: 'Earthquakes, and extraordinary commotions of the Seas. Then the darkness or bloudy colour of the Sun and Moon; The Shaking of the Powers of Heaven, the fulgurations of the Air and the falling of Stars.'[16] Thus, throughout the poem images from *Theory of the Earth* are regularly invoked:

> All in a hot and copper sky
> > The bloody sun at noon,
> Right up above the mast did stand,
> > No bigger than the moon.   (107–10)

[I]n some foggy days the Sun hangs in the Firmament as a lump of Bloud. And both the Sun and Moon at their rising, when their light comes to us through the thick vapours of the Earth, are red and fiery . . . (Burnet, *Theory of the Earth*, ii. 96)

> The upper air bursts into life,
> > And a hundred fire-flags sheen
> To and fro they are hurried about;
> And to and fro, and in and out
> > The stars dance on between.   (305–9)

No doubt there will be all sorts of fiery Meteors at that time . . . I think this expression does chiefly refer to Comets; which are dead Stars, and may truly be said to fall from heaven, when they leave their seats above, and those ethereal regions wherein they were fixt, and sink into this lower World; where they wander about with a blaze in their tail, or a flame about their head, as if they came on purpose to be the Messengers of some fiery Vengeance . . . (*Theory of the Earth*, ii. 98–9)

> The sun right up above the mast
> > Had fix'd her to the ocean:
> But in a minute she 'gan stir
> > With a short uneasy motion—
> Backwards and forward half her length
> > With a short uneasy motion.   (388–93)

---

[15] *Rights of Man*, 290.   [16] Burnet, *Theory of the Earth*, ii. 92–3.

Some Causes impelling the Waters one way, and some another, make intestine struglings and contrary motions; from whence proceed unusual noises, and such a troubled state of the Waters, as does not only make the Sea innavigable, but also strikes terror into all the Maritime inhabitants, that live within the sound or view of it . . . (*Theory of the Earth*, ii. 96)

> The Boat came close beneath the Ship,
>   And strait a sound was heard!
>
> Under the water it rumbled on,
>   Still louder and more dread:
> It reach'd the Ship, it split the bay;
>   The Ship went down like lead.   (577–82)

Next to Earth-quakes, we may consider the *roarings of a troubled Sea*. This is another sign of a dying World. . . . I do not look upon this ominous noise of the Sea, as the effect of a tempest, for then it would not strike such a terrour into the Inhabitants of the Earth, nor make them apprehensive of some great evil coming upon the World, as this will do, what proceeds from visible causes, and such as may happen in a common course of Nature, does not so much amaze us, nor affright us. Therefore 'tis more likely these disturbances of the Sea proceed from below . . . partly by Earth-quakes in the very Sea it self; with exhalations and fiery Eruptions from the bottom of it. . . . which make it roar, as it were, for pain . . . (*Theory of the Earth*, ii. 94–5)

The miraculous stanzas at the end of part 4 of *The Ancient Mariner* describe the new creative act of God which forms the millennial world. Seen as creatures of decay until this moment, the spontaneously generated 'slimy shapes' now appear as immature sea-snakes, held for the symbolic duration of the curse in the first stage of their life cycle. As the moon rises, it invigorates the ocean and evokes a glittering response in this young life. Coleridge had experienced such a moment:

—Hartley fell down & hurt himself—I caught him up crying & screaming— & ran out of doors with him. — The Moon caught his eye — he ceased crying immediately — & his eyes & the tears in them, how they glittered in the Moonlight! (CN i. 219)

Wherever the light of the moon falls the spell of the decaying burning sea is broken and life returns. The sea-snakes mature in the enlivened water, and as they disturb the myriads of luminescent larvae the water shines brightly:

> The moving Moon went up the sky
>   And no where did abide:
> Softly she was going up
>   And a star or two beside—
>
> Her beams bemock'd the sultry main
>   Like morning frosts yspread;
> But where the ship's huge shadow lay,
> The charmed water burnt alway
>   A still and awful red.
>
> Beyond the shadow of the ship
>   I watch'd the water-snakes:
> They mov'd in tracks of shining white;
> And when they rear'd the elfish light
>   Fell off in hoary flakes.   (255–68)

The light of the moon, like the breeze in *Joan of Arc*, transforms the uncreated parasites of a decaying ocean into protoplastic larval forms, imbued with vitality to grow and develop. For a few moments the phosphoreal oils burn in the ship's shadow where the moonlight cannot penetrate, but as the ocean begins to teem with life, the snakes fill the darkness with their own luminescence and dispel the redness of the corrupted water, as Night had been dispelled in *Joan of Arc*:

> Within the shadow of the ship
>   I watch'd their rich attire:
> Blue, glossy green, and velvet black
> They coil'd and swam; and every track
>   Was a flash of golden fire.   (269–73)

As the creative, living light at last overcomes the decaying fires around the spellbound ship, it elicits in the mariner an overflowing affirmation of life. At this moment of oneness between God and man, the burden of his old world is transformed by the plastic power of his imagination, and in place of death there is now life:

> O happy living things! no tongue
>   Their beauty might declare:
> A spring of love gusht from my heart,
>   And I bless'd them unaware!   (274–7)

Twenty years earlier, gazing on the marvellous sea-luminescence in the Cape of Good Hope from the deck of the *Resolution*, the young naturalist Georg Forster had concluded:

There was a singularity, and a grandeur in the display of this phaenomenon, which could not fail of giving occupation to the mind, and striking it with a reverential awe, due to Omnipotence. The ocean covered to a great extent, with myriads of animalcules; these little beings, organized alive, endowed with locomotive power, a quality of shining whenever they please, of illuminating every body with which they come in contact, and of laying aside their luminous appearance at pleasure: all these ideas crouded upon us, and bade us admire the Creator, even in his minutest works. It is the natural fault of young people to think too well of mankind; but I hope I shall not have formed too favourable an opinion of my readers, if I expect that the generality will sympathize with me in these feelings, and that none will be found ignorant or depraved enough to despise them. (*Voyage round the World*, i. 56–7)

Bibliography

Manuscripts

British Library:
  Egerton 2801
  Ashley 408
  Add. MS 35,343.
Humanities Research Center, University of Texas at Austin:
  'Rugby MS' (consulted on microfilm).

Primary Sources

'An Account of the Book entitled *Commercium Epistolicum Collinii et aliorum, De Analysi promota*; published by order of the *Royal-Society*, in relation to the Dispute between Mr. *Leibnitz* and Dr. *Keill*, about the Right of invention of the Method of *Fluxions*, by some call'd the *Differential Method*'. *Phil. Trans.* xxix (1714–16), 173–224.

AKENSIDE, MARK. *The Poems of Mark Akenside, M.D.* London, 1772.

BAXTER, ANDREW. *An Enquiry into the Nature of the Human Soul; wherein the Immateriality of the Soul Is evinced from the Principles of Reason and Philosophy*. London [1733]; 3rd edn., 2 vols., London, 1745.

BEDDOES, THOMAS. *A Letter to Erasmus Darwin, M.D. on a New Method of treating Pulmonary Consumption and some other Diseases hitherto found Incurable*. Bristol [1793].

—— and WATT, JAMES. *Considerations on the Medicinal Use of Factitious Airs, and on the manner of obtaining them in large quantities*. 2nd edn. Bristol, 1795–6.

BERKELEY, GEORGE. *The Works of George Berkeley, D.D. Late Bishop of Cloyne in Ireland*. 2 vols. London, 1784.

Philosophical Works of George Berkeley. Ed. M. Ayers. London, 1968.

BERTHELOT, MARCELIN. *La Révolution chimique: Lavoisier*. Paris, 1890.

BINET, ALFRED and FÉRÉ, CHARLES. *Animal Magnetism*. London, 1887.

BIRCH, THOMAS. *The History of the Royal Society of London, for improving of Natural Knowledge, from its first rise*. Vol. iii. London, 1757.

BLUMENBACH, JOHANN. *Über den Bildungstrieb das Zeugungsgeschäfte*. Gottingen, 1781. Trans. Andrew Crichton, *An Essay on Generation*. London [1792].

BOGUE, DAVID and BENNETT, JAMES. *History of Dissenters, from the Revolution in 1688, to the Year 1808*. 4 vols. London, 1808–12.

BOSCOVICH, ROGER. *Theoria Philosophiae Naturalis. Redacta ad unicam legem virium in natura existentium*. Venice, 1763. Trans. J. M. Child,

A Theory of Natural Philosophy. Chicago and London, 1922; reprinted Cambridge, Mass., 1966.

BOURZES, Father. 'A Letter from Father *Bourzes* to Father *Estienne Souciet*, concerning the *Luminous Appearance* observable in the *Wakes* of *Ships* in the *Indian Seas*'. *Phil. Trans.* xxviii (1713), 230–5.

BOWLES, WILLIAM. 'Coleridge a Private Soldier'. *Athenaeum*, cccliii (1834), 613; reprinted in R. and J. Haven and M. Adams (eds.), *Samuel Taylor Coleridge: An Annotated Bibliography of Criticism and Scholarship*, i: 1793–1899 (London, 1976), 80.

BOYLE ROBERT. *The Works of the Honourable Robert Boyle*. Ed. Thomas Birch. 2nd edn. 6 vols. London, 1772.

BURNET, THOMAS. *Telluris theoria sacra: orbis nostri originem et mutationes generales, quas aut iam subiit, aut olim subiturus est, complectens.* 2 vols. London, 1681, 1689.

—— *The Theory of the Earth, Containing an Account of the Original of the Earth, and of all the General Changes Which it hath already undergone, or is to undergo Till the Consummation of all Things.* 2 vols. London, 1684, 1690.

The Cambridge Intelligencer. Nos. 1–48: 20 July 1793–14 June 1794.

CAPPON, L.-J., ed. *The Adams-Jefferson Letters: The Complete Correspondence between Thomas Jefferson and Abigail and John Adams.* 2 vols. Chapel Hill, NC, 1959.

CASAUBON, ISAAC. *De rebus sacris et ecclesiasticis exercitationes xvi. Ad Cardinalis Baronii Prolegomena in Annales, et primam eorum partem, de Domini Nostri Iesu Christi nativitate, vita, passione, assumtione.* London, 1614.

COLERIDGE, SAMUEL T. *A Moral and Political Lecture, delivered at Bristol.* Bristol [1795].

—— *Conciones ad Populum. Or, Addresses to the People.* Bristol, 1795.

—— *The Plot Discovered; or, an Address to the People, against ministerial treason.* Bristol, 1795.

—— *An Answer to 'A Letter to Edward Long Fox, M.D.'* Bristol, 1795.

—— *Poems on Various Subjects.* London and Bristol, 1796.

—— *Poems, by S. T. Coleridge, Second Edition. To which are now added Poems by Charles Lamb, and Charles Lloyd.* London and Bristol, 1797.

—— *Sibylline Leaves: A Collection of Poems.* London, 1817.

—— *Biographia Literaria.* Ed. John Shawcross. 2 vols. Oxford, 1907.

—— [and SOUTHEY, ROBERT.] *The Fall of Robespierre. An historic drama.* Cambridge, 1794.

—— [and WORDSWORTH, WILLIAM.] *Lyrical Ballads, with a few other poems.* [London and Bristol] 1798.

Lyrical Ballads. The Text of the 1798 Edition with the Additional 1800 Poems and the Prefaces. Ed. R. L. Brett and A. R. Jones. London, 1963.

Coleridge: Poems. Ed. John Beer. London, 1963.

Collected Letters of Samuel Taylor Coleridge. Ed. Earl L. Griggs. 6 vols. Oxford, 1956–71.

The Collected Works of Samuel Taylor Coleridge. Bollingen Series, LXXV. General Editor Kathleen Coburn. i: *Lectures 1795 On Politics and Religion.* Ed. Lewis Patton and Peter Mann. London and Princeton, NJ, 1971. ii: *The Watchman.* Ed. Lewis Patton. London and Princeton, NJ, 1970. iv (2 parts): *The Friend* (1809–10, 1812, 1818). Ed. Barbara Rooke. London and Princeton, NJ, 1969.

The Complete Poetical Works of Samuel Taylor Coleridge. Ed. Ernest H. Coleridge. 2 vols. Oxford, 1912.

The Notebooks of Samuel Taylor Coleridge. Ed. Kathleen Coburn. 3 vols. London, 1957– .

COOK, JAMES and KING, JAMES. *A Voyage to the Pacific Ocean. Undertaken, by the Command of His Majesty for making Discoveries in the Northern Hemisphere.* 3 vols. London, 1784.

COOPER, THOMAS. *Some Information respecting America.* London, 1794.

[—— and Joseph Priestley, jun.] *Plan de Vente de Trois Cent Mille Acres de Terres Situées dans les Comtés de Northumberland et de Huntingdon dans L'État de Pensylvanie.* Paris, 1794.

COTTLE, JOSEPH. *Early Recollections; chiefly relating to the late Samuel Taylor Coleridge, during his long residence in Bristol.* 2 vols. Bristol, 1837.

CUDWORTH, RALPH. *The True Intellectual System of the Universe: The First Part; Wherein, All the Reason and Philosophy of Atheism is Confuted; and its Impossibility Demonstrated.* London, 1678 (Printed 1671). 2nd edn. Ed. Thomas Birch. 2 vols. London, 1743.

DAMASCIUS SYRUS. *Damascii philosophi Platonici Quaestiones de primis principiis.* Ed. C. A. Ruelle. 2 vols. Paris, 1889.

DARWIN, ERASMUS. *The Botanic Garden; A Poem, in Two Parts.* Vol. i, London, 1791; vol. ii, Litchfield, 1789.

—— *Zoonomia; or, The Laws of Organic Life.* 2 vols. London, 1794, 1796.

—— *The Temple of Nature; or, the Origin of Society; A Poem, with Philosophical Notes.* London, 1803.

The Letters of Erasmus Darwin. Ed. D. King-Hele. Cambridge, 1981.

DAVY, HUMPHRY. *The Collected Works of Sir Humphry Davy, Bart.* Ed. John Davy. 9 vols. London, 1839–40.

DIOGENES LAERTIUS. *Lives of Eminent Philosophers.* Trans. R. D. Hicks. 2 vols. London, 1925.

ENFIELD, WILLIAM. *The History of Philosophy, from the earliest times to the beginning of the present century, drawn up from Brückner's* Historia Critica Philosophiae. 2 vols. London, 1791.

EVELYN, JOHN. *The Diary of John Evelyn.* Ed. E. S. De Beer. 6 vols. Oxford, 1955.

FERRIAR, JOHN. 'Of Popular Illusion, and particularly of Medical Demonology'. *Memoirs of the Lit. & Phil.* iii (1790), 31–116 (misnumbered).

—— 'Observations concerning the Vital Principle'. *Memoirs of the Lit. & Phil.* iii (1790), 216–41.

—— 'An Argument against the Doctrine of Materialism, addressed to Thomas Cooper, Esq.' *Memoirs of the Lit. & Phil.* iv (1793), 20–44.

FORSTER, GEORGE. *A Voyage round the World, in His Britannic Majesty's Sloop, Resolution, commanded by Capt. James Cook, during the Years 1772, 3, 4, and 5.* 2 vols. London, 1777.

FORSTER, JOHN REINOLD. *Observations made during a voyage round the World, on Physical Geography, Natural History and Ethic Philosophy.* London, 1778.

[FOURCROY, ANTOINE DE]. *Notice sur la Vie et les Travaux de Lavoisier, précédée d'un discours sur les funérailles, et suivi d'une ode sur l'immortalité de l'âme.* Paris, l'an quatrième [1796].

FREND, WILLIAM. *Peace and Union recommended to the Associated Bodies of Republicans and Anti-Republicans.* St Ives, 1793.

GALVANI, LUIGI. *De Viribus Electricitatis in motu musculari commentarius.* Bologna, 1791. Trans. M. G. Foley, *Commentary on the Effects of Electricity on Muscular Motion.* Norwalk, Calif., 1953.

GUNNING, HENRY. *Reminiscences of the University, Town, and County of Cambridge, from the Year 1780.* 2 vols. London, 1854.

HARTLEY, DAVID. *Observations on Man, his Frame, his Duty, and his Expectations.* Ed. Herman A. Pistorius. 3 vols. London, 1791.

HARVEY, WILLIAM. *Anatomical Exercitations Concerning the Generation of Living Creatures: To which are added Particular Discourses, of Births, and of Conceptions, etc.* London, 1653.

HAYGARTH, JOHN. 'Description of a Glory'. *Memoirs of the Lit. & Phil.* iii (1790), 463–7.

HUNTER, JOHN. 'On the Digestion of the Stomach after Death'. *Phil. Trans.* lxii (1772), 447–54.

—— 'Anatomical Observations on the Torpedo'. *Phil. Trans.* lxiii (1773), 481–9.

—— 'An Account of the *Gymnotus Electricus*'. *Phil. Trans.* lxv (1775), 395–407.

—— 'Observations on the Structure and Oeconomy of *Whales*'. *Phil. Trans.* lxxvii (1787), 371–450.

—— *A Treatise on the Blood, Inflammation, and Gun-Shot Wounds.* London, 1794.

HUTTON, JAMES. *Theory of the Earth, with Proofs and Illustrations.* 2 vols. Edinburgh, 1795.

—— *Dissertations on Different Subjects in Natural Philosophy.* Edinburgh, 1792.

IAMBLICHUS CHALCIDENSIS. *De Mysteriis Aegyptiorum.* Ed. Thomas Gale. Oxford, 1678.

LAMB, CHARLES. *The Letters of Charles and Mary Ann Lamb.* Ed. E. W. Marrs, jun. 3 vols. Ithaca, NY and London, 1975– .

LAVOISIER, ANTOINE-LAURENT. *Traité Élémentaire de Chimie, présenté dans un ordre nouveau et d'après les découvertes modernes.* 2 vols. Paris, 1789. Trans. Robert Kerr, *Elements of Chemistry, in a new systematic order, containing all the modern discoveries.* Edinburgh, 1790; reprinted with intro. by D. Mackie, New York, 1965.

LOCKE, JOHN. *An Essay Concerning Human Understanding.* Ed. P. H. Nidditch. Oxford, 1975.

MACLAURIN, COLIN. *An Account of Sir Isaac Newton's Philosophical Discoveries.* London, 1748.

MEAD, RICHARD. *De imperio Solis ac Lunae in Corpora Humana et Morbis inde oriundis.* London, 1704. Trans. Thomas Stack, *A Treatise Concerning the Influence of the Sun and Moon upon Human Bodies, and the Diseases thereby produced.* London, 1748.

MESMER, ANTON. *Mémoire sur la découverte du Magnétisme Animal.* Geneva, 1779. Trans. V. R. Myers. London, 1948.

MONRO, ALEXANDER. *Observations on the Structure and Functions of the Nervous System.* Edinburgh, 1783.

MORE, HENRY. *Conjectura Cabbalistica. Or, A Conjectural Essay of Interpreting the Minde of Moses, according to a Threefold Cabbala.* London, 1653.

—— *The Immortality of the Soul.* London, 1659.

—— *A Collection of Several Philosophical Writings of Dr. Henry More.* 4th edn. London, 1712–13.

NEWTON, ISAAC. *Opticks Or A Treatise of the Reflexions, Refractions, Inflections and Colours of Light.* 2nd edn. London, 1717–18.

—— *Sir Isaac Newton's Mathematical Principles of Natural Philosophy and his System of the World.* Trans. Andrew Motte (London, 1729); rev. F. Cajori, Berkeley, Calif., 1934.

Isaaci Newtoni Opera Quae Exstant Omnia. Ed. Samuel Horsley. 5 vols. London, 1779–85.

The Correspondence of Isaac Newton. Ed. H. W. Turnbull. 7 vols. Cambridge, 1959–77.

OWEN, ROBERT. *The Life of Robert Owen: Written by Himself.* London, 1857.

PAINE, THOMAS. *Rights of Man.* Ed. H. Collins. London, 1969.

—— *The Age of Reason, Being An Investigation of True and of Fabulous Theology.* Part 1, 2nd edn., London, 1795; part 2, London, 1795.

PEMBERTON, HENRY. *A View of Sir Isaac Newton's Philosophy.* London, 1728.

PLATO. *The Republic*. Trans. P. Shorey. 2 vols. London and Harvard, 1930.

—— *Timaeus and Critias*. Trans. D. Lee. London, 1971.

Poetry of the Anti-Jacobin. London, 1799.

PRICE, RICHARD. *Observations on the Nature of Civil Liberty, the Principles of Government, and the Justice and Policy of the War with America*. 7th edn. London, 1776.

—— *Observations on the Importance of the American Revolution, and The Means of making it a Benefit to the World*. Rev. edn. London, 1785.

PRIESTLEY, JOSEPH. *The History and Present State of Electricity, with Original Experiments*. London, 1767.

—— *An Essay on the First Principles of Government; and on the nature of political, civil, and religious liberty*. London, 1768.

—— *The History and Present State of Discoveries relating to Vision, Light, and Colours*. 2 vols. London, 1772.

—— 'Observations on different Kinds of Air'. *Phil. Trans.* lxii (1772), 147–264.

—— *Experiments and Observations on Different Kinds of Air*. 3 vols. London, 1774–7.

—— *Hartley's Theory of the Human Mind, on the principle of the Association of Ideas; with Essays relating to the subject of it*. London, 1775.

—— *Disquisitions Relating to Matter and Spirit. To which is added, the history of the philosophical doctrine concerning the origin of the soul, and the nature of matter; with its influence on Christianity, etc.* London, 1777.

—— *Experiments and Observations relating to various branches of Natural Philosophy, with a continuation of the Observations on Air*. 3 vols. London, 1779–86.

—— *The present State of Europe compared with Antient Prophecies; A Sermon, preached at The Gravel Pit Meeting in Hackney, February 28, 1794, Being the Day appointed for a General Fast*. London, 1794.

—— 'Observations and Experiments relating to Equivocal or Spontaneous Generation'. *Trans. Amer. Phil. Soc.* vi (1806), 119–26.

—— *Memoirs of Dr. Joseph Priestley, to the year 1795, written by himself; with a continuation, to the time of his decease, by his son, Joseph Priestley; and observations on his writings, By Thomas Cooper, President Judge of the 4th District of Pennsylvania; and the Rev. William Christie*. 2 vols. London, 1806–7.

The Theological and Miscellaneous Works, etc., of Joseph Priestley, LL.D. F.R.S. etc. with notes, by the editor. Ed. John T. Rutt. 25 vols. London, 1817–31.

PRINGLE, JOHN. *A Discourse on the different kinds of Air, delivered at the anniversary of the Royal Society, Nov. 30, 1773*. London, 1774.

RAMSAY, ANDREW. *The Philosophical Principles of Natural and Revealed Religion.* 2 vols. Glasgow, 1748–9.

'A Relation of an extraordinary effect of the power of Imagination: Communicated by Mr. *Edward Smith*, Secretary to the Philosophical Society at *Dublin*, as it was brought before that Company, by Mr. *St. George Ash, R. Soc. S.* who had seen the thing'. *Phil. Trans.* xvi (1686–92), 334.

Report of Dr. Benjamin Franklin, and other Commissioners, charged by the King of France, with the Examination of the Animal Magnetism, as now practised at Paris. London, 1785.

ROCHEFOUCAULD-LIANCOURT, FRANÇOIS, Duc de. *Voyage dans les États-Unis D'Amérique, fait en 1795, 1796 et 1797.* 8 vols. Paris, l'An vii de la République [1799].

ROUSSEAU, JEAN-JACQUES. *A Discourse on Inequality.* Trans. M. Cranston. Harmondsworth, 1984.

SNOW, CHARLES P. *The Two Cultures and the Scientific Revolution.* Cambridge, 1959.

SOUTHEY, CHARLES (ed.). *The Life and Correspondence of Robert Southey.* 6 vols. London, 1849–50.

SOUTHEY, ROBERT. *Joan of Arc, An Epic Poem.* Bristol, 1796.

The Correspondence of Robert Southey with Caroline Bowles. Ed. Edward Dowden. London, 1881.

SPALLANZANI, Abbé LAZARO. *Dissertazioni di fisica animale e vegetabile.* Modena, 1780. Trans. Thomas Beddoes, *Dissertations relative to the Natural History of Animals and Vegetables.* 2nd edn. 2 vols. London, 1789.

STOCK, JOHN. *Memoirs of the Life of Thomas Beddoes, M.D. with an analytical account of his writings.* London, 1811.

SULIVAN, RICHARD. *A View of Nature, in Letters to a Traveller among the Alps. With Reflections on Atheistical Philosophy, now exemplified in France.* 6 vols. London, 1794.

THELWALL, JOHN. *An Essay towards a definition of Animal Vitality; read at the Theatre, Guy's Hospital, January 26, 1793; in which several of the opinions of the Celebrated John Hunter are examined and controverted.* London [1793]

THOMAS, DYLAN. *Collected Poems 1934–1952.* London, 1952.

THOMSON, JAMES. *The Complete Poetical Works.* Ed. J. L. Robertson. Oxford, 1908.

VOLTAIRE. *Letters Concerning the English Nation.* Trans. J. Lockman. London, 1733.

WAKEFIELD, GILBERT. *The Spirit of Christianity, compared with the Spirit of the Times in Great Britain.* London, 1794.

WALES, WILLIAM. *Remarks on Mr. Forster's account of Capt. Cook's last Voyage round the World in the years 1772, 1773, 1774, and 1775.* London, 1778.

WESLEY, JOHN. *The Desideratum: or, Electricity Made Plain and Useful.* London, 1760.

WORDSWORTH, WILLIAM. *The Prelude 1799, 1805, 1850.* Ed. J. Wordsworth, M. H. Abrahams, and S. Gill. New York and London, 1979.

Secondary Sources

BARFIELD, O. *What Coleridge Thought.* Oxford, 1972.

BARNES, J. *The PreSocratic Philosophers.* 2 vols. London, 1979.

BEER, J. *Coleridge the Visionary.* London, 1959.

—— *Coleridge's Poetic Intelligence.* London, 1977.

CANTOR, G. N. and HODGE, M. J. S. (eds.). *Conceptions of Ether: Studies in the History of Ether Theories 1740–1900.* Cambridge, 1981.

CASSIRER, E. *Die platönische Renaissance in England und die Schule von Cambridge.* Leipzig and Berlin, 1932. Trans. J. P. Pettegrove, *The Platonic Renaissance in England.* Edinburgh, 1953.

CHADWICK, H. 'Philo and the Beginnings of Christian Thought', in A. H. Armstrong (ed.), *The Cambridge History of Later Greek and Early Medieval Philosophy.* Cambridge, 1967, pp. 133–92.

COBURN, K. 'Coleridge: A Bridge between Science and Poetry', in J. Beer (ed.), *Coleridge's Variety: Bicentenary Studies.* London, 1974, pp. 81–100.

COHEN, I. B. *Franklin and Newton: An Inquiry into Speculative Newtonian Experimental Science and Franklin's Work in Electricity as an Example Thereof.* Philadelphia, Pa., 1956.

—— 'The Eighteenth-Century Origins of the Concept of Scientific Revolution', *JHI* xxxvii (1976), 257–88.

CRANE, V. W. 'The Club of Honest Whigs: Friends of Science and Liberty'. *William and Mary Quarterly*, 3rd ser., xxiii (1966), 210–33.

DARNTON, R. *Mesmerism and the End of the Enlightenment in France.* Cambridge, Mass., 1968.

FARLEY, J. *The Spontaneous Generation Controversy from Descartes to Operin.* Baltimore, Md., 1977.

FESTUGIÈRE, A.-J. *La Révélation d'Hèrmes Trismégiste.* 3rd edn. Vol. i. Paris, 1950.

FRUMAN, N. *Coleridge: The Damaged Archangel.* New York, 1971.

GOODWIN, A. *The Friends of Liberty: The English Democratic Movement in the Age of the French Revolution.* London, 1979.

GRIMAUX, E. *Lavoisier 1743–1794.* Paris, 1888.

GUERLAC, H. *Lavoisier: The Crucial Year.* Ithaca, NY, 1961.

GUTHRIE, W. K. C. 'The Early Presocratics and the Pythagoreans', in id. (ed.), *A History of Greek Philosophy*, Vol. i. Cambridge, 1962.

HARRISON, J. *The Library of Isaac Newton.* Cambridge, 1978.

HARRISON, J. F. C. *The Second Coming: Popular Millenarianism 1780–1850.* London, 1979.

HARVEY, E. N. *A History of Luminescence: From the Earliest Times until 1900*. Philadelphia, Pa., 1957.

HATCH, R. B. 'Joseph Priestley: An Addition to Hartley's *Observations*'. *JHI* xxxvi (1975), 548–50.

HAVEN, R. 'Coleridge, Hartley, and the Mystics'. *JHI* xx (1959), 477–94.

—— HAVEN, J. and ADAMS, M. (eds.). *Samuel Taylor Coleridge: An Annotated Bibliography of Criticism and Scholarship*. Vol. i: 1793–1899. London, 1976.

HEIMANN, P. M. and McGUIRE, J. E. 'Newtonian Forces and Lockean Powers: Concepts of Matter in Eighteenth-Century Thought'. *Historical Studies in the Physical Sciences* iii (1971), 233–306.

HILL, J. S. *A Coleridge Companion*. London, 1983.

JACOB, M. C. and LOCKWOOD, W. A. 'Political Millenarianism and Burnet's Sacred Theory'. *Science Studies*, ii (1972), 265–79.

KELLEY, M. W. 'Thomas Cooper and Pantisocracy'. *Modern Language Notes*, xlv (1930), 218–20.

KNIGHT, D. M. 'The Vital Flame', *Ambix*, xxiii (1976), 5–15.

KNIGHT, F. *The Strange Case of Thomas Walker: Ten Years in the Life of a Manchester Radical*. London, 1957.

—— *University Rebel: The Life of William Frend (1757–1841)*. London, 1971.

LESLIE, M. 'Mysticism Misunderstood: David Hartley and the Idea of Progress'. *JHI* xxxiii (1972), 625–32.

LEVERE, T. H. 'Dr Thomas Beddoes and the Establishment of his Pneumatic Institution: A Tale of Three Presidents'. *Notes and Records of the Royal Society of London*, xxxii (1977), 41–9.

—— 'S. T. Coleridge and the Human Sciences: Anthropology, Phrenology, and Mesmerism', in M. P. Hanen, M. J. Osler, and R. G. Weyant (eds.), *Science, Pseudo-Science and Society*. Waterloo, NY, 1980, pp. 171–92.

—— *Poetry Realized in Nature: Samuel Taylor Coleridge and Early Nineteenth-Century Science*. Cambridge, 1981.

LINCOLN, A. *Some Political and Social Ideas of English Dissent 1763–1800*. Cambridge, 1938.

LITCHFIELD, R. B. *Tom Wedgwood: The First Photographer*. London, 1903.

LOEMKER, L. E. 'Monad and Monadology', in P. Edwards (ed.), *The Encyclopedia of Philosophy*. Vol. v, London and New York, 1967, pp. 361–3.

LOVEJOY, A. O. *The Great Chain of Being: A Study of the History of an Idea*. Cambridge, Mass., 1936.

LOWES, J. L. *The Road to Xanadu: A Study in the Ways of the Imagination*. 2nd edn. New York, 1930; reprinted Boston, Mass., 1955.

McEvoy, J. G. 'Joseph Priestley, "Aerial Philosopher": Metaphysics and Methodology in Priestley's Chemical Thought, from 1772 to 1781'. *Ambix*, xxv (1978), 1–55, 93–116, 153–75; ibid. xxvi (1979), 16–38.

McFarland, T. *Coleridge and the Pantheist Tradition*. Oxford, 1969.

MacGillivray, J. R. 'The Pantisocracy Scheme and its Immediate Background', in M. W. Wallace (ed.), *Studies in English by Members of University College Toronto*. Toronto, 1931, pp. 131–69.

McGuire, J. E. 'Force, Active Principles, and Newton's Invisible Realm'. *Ambix*, xv (1968), 154–208.

Martin, C. G. 'Coleridge and Cudworth: A Source for "The Eolian Harp"'. *Notes and Queries*, ccxi (1966), 173–6.

Murphy, M. J. *Cambridge Newspapers and Opinion, 1789–1850*. Cambridge, 1977.

Oliver, W. H. *Prophets and Millennialists: The Uses of Biblical Prophecy in England from the 1790s to the 1840s*. Auckland and Oxford, 1978.

Pagel, W. *William Harvey's Biological Ideas*. New York, 1967.

Pattie, F. A. 'Mesmer's Medical Dissertation and Its Debt to Mead's *De Imperio Solis ac Lunae*', *J. Hist. Med.* xi (1956), 275–87.

Piper, H. W. *The Active Universe: Pantheism and the Concept of Imagination in the English Romantic Poets*. London, 1962.

—— ' "The Eolian Harp" Again'. *Notes and Queries*, ccxiii (1968), 23–5.

Ritterbush, P. C. *Overtures to Biology: The Speculations of Eighteenth-Century Naturalists*. New Haven, Conn. and London, 1964.

Robinson, E. 'An English Jacobin: James Watt, junior, 1769–1848'. *Cambridge Historical Journal*, xi (1955), 349–55.

—— 'The Origins and Life-Span of the Lunar Society'. *Univ. Birm. Hist. J.* xi (1967), 5–16.

Rogers, G. A. J. 'Locke, Newton, and the Cambridge Platonists on Innate Ideas'. *JHI* xl (1979), 191–205.

Sailor, D. B. 'Moses and Atomism'. *JHI* xxv (1964), 3–16; reprinted in C. A. Russell (ed.), *Science and Religious Belief*, London, 1973, pp. 5–19.

Schofield, R. E. *The Lunar Society of Birmingham: A Social History of Provincial Science and Industry in Eighteenth-Century England*. Oxford, 1963.

—— 'The Lunar Society and the Industrial Revolution'. *Univ. Birm. Hist. J.* xi (1967), 94–119.

Smith, B. 'Coleridge's *Ancient Mariner* and Cook's Second Voyage'. *J. Warburg & Courtauld Inst.* xix (1956), 117–54.

Stephens, F. C. 'Cottle, Wise and *MS Ashley 408*'. *Bibliographical Society of America Papers*, lxviii (1974), 391–406.

Thomas, D. O. *The Honest Mind: The Thought and Work of Richard Price*. Oxford, 1977.

UNSWORTH, J. 'Coleridge and the Manchester Academy'. *Charles Lamb Bulletin*, NS xxx (1980), 149–53.

WALKER, D. P. *The Ancient Theology: Studies in Christian Platonism from the Fifteenth to the Eighteenth Century*. London, 1972.

WALLIS, R. T. *Neo-platonism*. London, 1972.

WESTFALL, R. S. *Never at Rest: A Biography of Isaac Newton*. Cambridge, 1980.

WHALLEY, GEORGE. 'The Bristol Library Borrowings of Southey and Coleridge, 1793–98'. *The Library*, 5th ser., iv (1949), 114–32.

WHEELER, K. M. *The Creative Mind in Coleridge's Poetry*. London, 1981.

WILLEY, B. *The Seventeenth-Century Background: Studies in the Thought of the Age in Relation to Poetry and Religion*. London, 1934.

—— *Nineteenth-Century Studies*. London, 1949.

WOOF, R. 'Wordsworth and Coleridge: Some Early Matters', in J. Wordsworth (ed.), *Bicentenary Wordsworth Studies in Memory of John Alban Finch*. Ithaca, NY, 1970, pp. 76–91.

YATES, F. A. *Giordano Bruno and the Hermetic Tradition*. London, 1964.

YOUNG, R. 'The Life Within: *The Prelude* and Organic Form'. Oxford Univ. D. Phil. thesis, 1980.

ZALL, P. M. 'The Cool World of Samuel Taylor Coleridge: Up Loyal Sock Creek'. *Wordsworth Circle*, iii (1972), 161–7.

Index